INDO-PAK CONFLICTS RIPE TO RESOLVE?

The Regional Centre for Strategic Studies (RCSS) is an independent, non-profit and non-governmental organization for collaborative research, networking and interaction on strategic and international issues pertaining to South Asia. Set up in 1992, the RCSS is based in Colombo, Sri Lanka.

The RCSS is a South Asian forum for studies, training and multi-track dialogue and deliberation on issues of regional interest. All activities of RCSS are designed with a South Asia focus and are usually participated by experts from all South Asian countries. The Centre is envisaged as a forum for advancing the cause of cooperation, security, conflict resolution, confidence building, peace and development in the countries of the South Asian region.

The RCSS serves its South Asian and international constituency by: (a) networking programmes that promote interaction, communication and exchange between institutions and individuals within and outside the region engaged in South Asian strategic studies; (b) organizing regional workshops and seminars and sponsoring and coordinating collaborative research; and (c) disseminating output of the research through publications which include books, monographs and a quarterly newsletter. The RCSS facilitates scholars and other professionals of South Asia to address, mutually and collectively, problems and issues of topical interest for all countries of the region.

Queries may be addressed to:

Regional Centre for Strategic Studies
2 Elibank Road
Colombo 5
SRI LANKA
Tel: (94-11) 2599734, 2599735
Fax: 2599993; e-mail: rcss@sri.lanka.net
RCSS website: http://www.rcss.org

RCSS Policy Studies 34

Indo-Pak Conflicts Ripe to Resolve?

RIZWAN ZEB
SUBA CHANDRAN

REGIONAL CENTRE FOR STRATEGIC STUDIES
COLOMBO

MANOHAR
2005

Published by
Ajay Kumar Jain for
Manohar Publishers & Distributors
4753/23 Ansari Road, Daryaganj
New Delhi 110 002
and
Regional Centre for Strategic Studies
2 Elibank Road
Colombo 5
SRI LANKA
Tel: (94-11) 2599734-5; Fax: 2599993;
e-mail: rcss@sri.lanka.net
Website: http://www.rcss.org

First published 2005

ISBN 81-7304-651-4

Typeset by
Kohli Print
Delhi 110 051

Printed at
Lordson Publishers Pvt. Ltd.
Delhi 110 007

Distributed in South Asia by
FOUNDATION
BOOKS
4381/4, Ansari Rorad
Daryaganj, New Delhi 110 002
and its branches at Mumbai, Hyderabad,
Bangalore, Chennai, Kolkata

Contents

RCSS is grateful to the
Ford Foundation for its generous
support for the Mahbub-ul-Haq Award
on which this report is based.

Foreword

As this important study is being published we are in the midst of a new round of the normalization process between South Asia's two major powers. We have reason to be optimistic, because this round involves more than official 'Track I' talks, but includes both Track II and extensive people-to-people diplomacy as well as a very welcome and long-overdue movement of Indians and Pakistanis across their common border for sporting, cultural and academic events. Therefore, this study is both timely and significant.

It is timely because it may well help India and Pakistan inch forward in the current 'peace process'. It sets forth both theoretical and practical guidelines on how to deal with what has long been recognized as a 'hurting stalemate'—a situation in which neither side can change the status quo by force, and all sides suffer to one degree or another.

This study begins with a careful review of conflict resolution literature, especially that part of it which deals with the problem of when a conflict might be 'ripe' for resolution, and applies the abstract lessons to the real world of South Asia.

The study is also significant in its own right because it is the product of two young and promising scholars from India (Chandran) and Pakistan (Zeb), under the auspices of South Asia's only regional centre devoted to the analysis and resolution of strategic conflict. The two authors met at an RCSS workshop, they conceived this jointly-written and researched study, and they are to be praised for its comprehensive and balanced assessment.

Because of their different background, they are especially sensitive to the importance of diverse perceptions of both the Kashmir issue and the larger context of India-Pakistan relations. As they note, there have been very different perceptions of 'ripeness' in New Delhi and Islamabad, with the relationship often resembling a psychological teeter-totter, one side up, the other down, and each side engrossed in calculating which way the advantage will swing in the next round.

This study also explores the different factors in South Asia that might make the India-Pakistan dispute ripe for resolution. One of these is the role of domestic politics in calculating whether to continue negotiations. As they point out, the current round was initiated when India's Prime Minister Atal Behari Vajpayee calculated that negotiations with Pakistan might help the BJP in a forthcoming election. This is new, but would a failed peace process turn the Indian (or Pakistani) public against further talks? Chandran and Zeb also explore the military dimensions of the strategic stalemate, its high economic costs, and the role that the Kashmiri people, separatists, and militants now play in the current round of talks.

Finally, the authors offer a set of innovative and realistic policy suggestions. These include the creation of joint consultative groups (to work around the heavy hand of bureaucracies), and a discussion of alternative arrangements for Kashmir, the importance of expanded people-to-people contacts, and the critical role that expanded trade might play in firming up any movement on the diplomatic front.

To some degree the fifty-year plus India-Pakistan stalemate has been ruinous to both countries. They may, or may not, climb the mountain in this round, but this study offers insights and ideas about the process, and should be read carefully by those directly involved. It represents the voice of a new and informed generation of Indian and Pakistani strategic thinkers, in this case working together to understand how their countries have found themselves in this hurting stalemate, and offering sound ideas as to how to extract themselves from it. The authors, and RCSS are to be commended for making this outstanding study available to a wider audience.

March 2005 STEPHEN P. COHEN

Preface

Everything has a beginning. Though in the words of a famous poet what we think is the beginning is often the end and the end is often the beginning. The idea of this work germinated at the Department of Peace and Conflict Research of the Uppsala University, Sweden, where one of the authors attended a course on International Conflict Studies in 2002 and came across the ripeness theory. The idea of undertaking a study on ripeness theory and linking it to the India-Pakistan conflict became stronger and we were looking for a fellowship which would enable us to carry out the study. Time seemed ripe for a joint study; we were fortunate to receive the Mahbub-ul-Haq fellowship of the Regional Centre for Strategic Studies, Colombo, Sri Lanka.

It was a good beginning, regardless of the troubles that followed. As long as the idea of a joint study remained in our thoughts, we presumed it would be easier to write. But only when we got going, we realized how wrong our presumptions were. One, the events between India and Pakistan were moving at such a fast pace since 2002, that we found it extremely difficult to race along with them. It was so fast that at times, our draft became outdated even before we could share it with each other. At times there were many false starts at the bilateral level, but we kept waiting for something to happen for the better.

Two, the more we started changing drafts, the more we realized how differently we perceived the same events. Agreed, that an event could be interpreted, depending on from which side we were looking at it, but at times we faced differences in what is considered to be a 'fact'. Especially on 'events' and 'facts' relating to Kashmir we had many differences; and they remain even today. We may not agree with each other, but we understand the perceptions and positions of each other.

Three, both of us were/are working with different institutions

(Institute of Peace and Conflict Studies, New Delhi and Institute of Regional Studies, Islamabad) and had other engagements. It is not that we considered this work secondary, but we had to look after our other responsibilities in the respective institutes. Perhaps it is the same case with India and Pakistan, where the leadership has to look at various issues, and India-Pakistan relations is one of them, albeit the most important one.

We would like to emphasize to the readers however that though this is a consensus study; it may not be an ideal one. We did not attempt to change each other's views, yet we were looking for a common ground where we could reach a consensus. We did and do have our differences; yet instead of insisting on one's interpretation, we were eager to compare notes about each other's perception and viewpoint. Perhaps, this itself can be seen as an achievement.

On the positive side, we were fortunate to be encouraged and inspired by some of the leading scholars both inside and outside South Asia. There were four pillars, who really supported us and our study during the last three years. General Jamshed Ayaz Khan and Professor P.R. Chari were supportive of the joint study, right from its inception. From the initial stages of sending the proposal and throughout the study, they supported us in many ways. Professor Stephen Philip Cohen, who was kind enough to write the foreword, was a great source of encouragement, guidance and criticism. In the last three years, he invited both of us to the Brookings Institution, at different periods and one of us was even more fortunate to be there for a longer period during the summer of 2004. He went through the drafts more than thrice during this period, giving us critical inputs. It was professionally satisfying and rewarding, to be able to closely associate with two of whom we consider as *C-3* (Chari, Cheema and Cohen) and who have greatly inspired and motivated us with their joint scholarly contributions. Our desire is to meet up with their excellent efforts—perhaps in the near future. Professor Sridhar Khatri, Director of the Regional Centre for Strategic Studies (RCSS), who was very keen on getting the best out of us, gave us time tc complete the study, in spite of his own deadlines. We should have submitted our drafts much earlier, but were able to do so in February 2005. He also gave us the crucial platform to meet each other and invited us to a workshop at Shanghai in 2003, which helped us greatly during the initial phase of our research.

Many other scholars helped us in providing vital inputs at various levels. Dr Moonis Ahmer, Ms Amera Saeed, Dr Rodney Jones and Dr Marvin Weinbaum in particular went through different sections, commenting and suggesting ways to further improve it. Professor Clifford Singer and Dr Matt Rosenstein at the ACDIS, University of Illinois, helped us to discuss sections of this study with a wider audience both inside and outside Urbana-Champaign. Maria Saifuddin Effendi, a bright young Pakistani scholar assisted us, especially with her crucial contributions to the theoretical sections. In addition, there were also vital comments and observations from an anonymous reviewer, to whom Professor Sridhar Khatri had sent the draft. Ms Minna Thaheer, Research Officer at the RCSS was continuously in touch with both of us throughout the study; always chasing us and keeping our study on track. We owe so much to their contributions.

We received help directly and indirectly from many other sources. In Pakistan, Dr Rifaat Hussian, former chair and professor at the Department of Defence and Strategic Studies at the Quaid-i-Azam University, Islamabad, currently senior fellow at the Institute for Strategic Studies Research and Analysis (ISSRA) of the National Defence College, Islamabad remains a mentor and friend. Brigadier (Retd) Bashir Ahmed has been a great source of guidance, support and encouragement and was instrumental in one of us making a career in the security studies. In India, Major General Dipankar Banerji, currently the Director of Institute of Peace and Conflict Studies, New Delhi was kind enough to organize a discussion on the draft, where there were numerous inputs and questions both on the theory and the subject matter.

Finally a small note on the sources that have been quoted or consulted in this study. Since, two of us have been engaged in research, it needs to be mentioned that one of us may not agree or at times even have read some of the sources in full detail. In most cases, where there have been differences of opinion, we have provided two different sources. There may have been some technical lapses, though we were extremely cautious and concerned about linking our statements and facts with correct sources. The authors alone are responsible for any errors, misjudgements, mischaracterizations, or other inaccuracies that may persist in this study.

March 2005

RIZWAN ZEB
SUBA CHANDRAN

Introduction

The peaceful resolution of conflicts is a highly commendable phenomenon in contemporary world politics. Theorists lay greater emphasis on different techniques to manage and resolve conflicts. Among popular theories of conflict resolution, the 'ripeness theory' deserves a thorough discussion to explore meaningful ways of crisis management and conflict resolution. The concept of ripe moment implies a situation whereby two conflicting parties view their respective positions in an impasse that hurts both parties. William Zartman, the pioneer of 'ripeness theory', terms the 'Mutually Hurting Stalemate' (MHS).

The moment *tends to be ripened* because an urgent need to resolve conflict is felt by the concerned parties. He argues that 'when the parties find themselves locked in a conflict from which they cannot escalate to victory and this deadlock is painful to both of them (although not necessarily in equal degrees or for the same reasons), they seek a way out'.[1]

The parties to the conflict according to Zartman, may feel the pain of the mutually hurting stalemate at the same time, but not necessarily at the same level. They calculate the costs of conflict (paid by them) and the benefits of peace (in the days ahead). In other words, when two parties to a conflict realize that they pay heavily and gain nothing by engaging in a crisis or warlike situation, they look for alternate options. Saliently, a ripe moment comprises three elements; gains and losses, deadlock and realization of this deadlock by the parties.

India and Pakistan, in this context, have been experiencing such impasses for a long time. Apparently, they seized the moment and tried to seek the suggested way out (negotiations) but could

[1] I.A. William Zartman, 'Ripeness: The Hurting Stalemate and Beyond', at <http://www.nap.edu/books/0309070279/html/225.html>

not reconcile their mutual differences. India and Pakistan are signatories to numerous accords and agreements. They have experienced different modes and techniques of conflict management and resolution (for instance bilateral negotiations, mediation, arbitration, etc.). None of these measures have helped them resolve their differences.

Why could not they settle their conflicts amicably? What factors did impinge on conflict resolution? Does MHS model suggest any particular conditions and ways through which conflicting parties can seek a way out permanently? How far is the MHS model is relevant to an Indo-Pak conflict? Are the Indo-Pak conflicts, including Kashmir ripe for resolution? What if the MHS fails to create ripe conditions in an Indo-Pak context? In the event of MHS failing to create ripeness, can it be created artificially through specific efforts at the civil society level, so that it could facilitate the two parties—the states of India and Pakistan to reach an understanding?

The study tries to answer these basic questions and seeks:

- To discuss the main components of Zartman's ripeness theory.
- To establish a relevant link of the theory with Indo-Pak conflicts.
- To find out whether the Indo-Pak conflicts including Kashmir are ripe for resolution.
- To suggest ways in which civil society could facilitate the State in India and Pakistan to reach an understanding out of their MHS.

CHAPTER 1

Ripeness and India-Pakistan Conflicts: In Search of a Framework

Zartman's ripeness theory suggests a right time to begin negotiations to resolve differences between or among the conflicting parties. At its core is the stalemate—a situation that neither assures a victory in military confrontation nor guarantees success in future. Scholars view the ripe moment in different ways. Mitchell gathers four prime models, related to ripe moment to resolve the acute differences between or among the parties.[1] Two initial models have been taken from Zartman's ripeness theory. These include: the Hurting Stalemate Model; the Imminent Mutual Catastrophe Model; the Entrapment Model; and the Enticing Opportunity Model. As mentioned earlier, the Hurting Stalemate Model suggests the same way that Zartman explains: *A hurting stalemate + realization of the deadlock = ripe moment for resolution.*

Similarly, the imminent catastrophe (another Zartmanian expression) delineates that parties only go for a peaceful way of resolution if they definitely feel the threat of an imminent disaster. This preconceived threat that 'both parties facing undeniable disaster, a huge increase in costs, and/or a major drop in the perceived probability of success and victory through continuing the struggle'[2] results in a situation that prevents the parties from intense military competition. Thus what makes the model highly questionable is whether the parties perceive the imminent catas-

[1] For details, see Christopher R. Mitchell, 'Cutting Losses: Reflections on Appropriate Timing', ICAR Working Paper 9, January 1996, <http://www.ciaonet.org/wps/mic01>

[2] For details, see Mitchell, 'Cutting Losses: Reflections on Appropriate Timing', p. 4.

trophe at the same time, with the same degree of realization or not. One man's victory is another man's defeat. If one party surmises the losses of the catastrophe on its side, the other party may not find the situation equally critical for itself. The element of 'mutuality' holds significant importance in this model.

With a psychological and political orientation, the entrapment model concludes that parties are fascinated to be engaged in continuing conflict. They view the cost they pay as 'investment' that further leads them towards ultimate victory. 'The greater the hurt, the more the need to continue towards 'victory' in order to justify both the psychological and political sacrifices already made.'[3]

Mitchell's fourth model proposes a positive and optimistic vision. It suggests that parties evaluate rewards and new benefits that they are supposed to gain in the absence of the prevalent tense environment. Supportive to Zartman's MHS model, Mooradian and Druckman analyse the link of mediation with ripe conditions.[4] They have produced a balanced assessment regarding the role of mediation in the Nagorno-Karabakh conflict (1990–5), in which they sum up that a third party cannot help the warring parties to seek a way out prior to severe skirmishes between them. This is what Mooradian and Druckman try to verify in terms of the Nagorno-Karabakh issue, 'the conflict over Nagorno-Karabakh prior to the offensives was not viewed by the parties as being sufficiently costly to encourage them to seek a way out through a mediated settlement. When the costs increased the parties found a way out by negotiating a settlement without the help of mediation.'[5]

They term the MHS as a perceptual concept according to which 'without acknowledging the existence of a stalemate, the parties

[3] Ibid., p. 5.

[4] For details see Moorad Mooradian and Daniel Druckman, 'Hurting Stalemate or Mediation? The Conflict over Nagorno-Karabakh, 1990–5', *Journal for Peace Research*, vol. 36, no. 6, pp. 712–13.

[5] For details see Moorad Mooradian and Daniel Druckman, 'Hurting Stalemate or Mediation? The Conflict over Nagorno-Karabakh, 1990–5', *Journal for Peace Research*, vol. 36, no. 6, p. 724.

are unlikely to change their behaviour from pursuing combat to peaceful relations.'[6]

Contrary to the above mentioned notion of the ripe moment (for conflict resolution) by different scholars, Steinberg gives a rational critique of the subject. He treats his exemplary data (case study of the Oslo Peace Process) with reference to the ripeness theory. According to his analysis, 'the main psychological elements, such as mutual understanding, empathy, 'relationship building', and trust are difficult to measure consistently and meaningfully at the societal level'.[7] He considers the Oslo Peace Process a failure because:

- The element of track two and track three diplomacy was missing, there was no people-to-people contact or intercultural, social or economic dialogue throughout the peace process.
- Mirror images could not be eliminated despite diplomatic efforts at the official level.
- Psychological foundations were weak at the societal level.

These three elements are the basis to the realization of ripe conditions. He, therefore suggests structural confidence building measures (CBMs at the grassroot level) to make the moment ripe to initiate a peace dialogue. He say, 'Common interests and mutual interdependencies in specific practical areas are developed which make increased conflict costly and undesirable to both sides'.[8]

Containg a detailed account of ripeness theory with different perspectives, the paper entails certain contradictory points and questions that make the discussions rather interesting. These are:

- Ripeness requires certain elements; for example, inter-party and intra-party realization of a deadlock on both sides. Inter-

[6] Ibid.

[7] Gerald M. Steinberg, 'Unripeness and Conflict Management: Re-examining the Oslo Process and its Lessons', <http://faculty.biu.ac.il/~steing/conflict/papers/re-examiningoslo.pdf>

[8] Steinberg, 'Unripeness and Conflict Management: Re-examining the Oslo Process and its Lessons', p. 8.

party refers to the consent of the governing elites (of both conflicting groups) who involve in the pre-ripeness as well as post-ripeness process directly. Intra-party realization indicates conviction by power elites who do not hold the power in actual terms but are influential in decision-making process.

- Whether the issue/conflict (upon which parties are quarreling against each other) is ripe for resolution or not. Sometimes, an issue perceived to be ripe by one party but not so by the other. This makes it controversial and leads them nowhere. Parties to the conflict should know and recognize the 'core' of their differences.
- Can a third party play a role in creating conditions for 'motivational ripeness'?

CHAPTER 2

Ripeness Theory and India-Pakistan Conflicts

Ever since their independence in 1947, the relations between India and Pakistan have been in a state of flux. They have had overt military conflicts on differing scales and close military confrontations in 1948, 1965, 1971, 1986–7, 1999 and 2002. There has been numerous unsuccessful attempts and meetings between the two countries at the highest levels to resolve the conflict. Why have India and Pakistan failed to resolve their conflict? What are the major factors that obstruct both countries leading towards a resolution? Do Indo-Pak conflicts share any parallel with others? Have there been any success stories elsewhere? Are there any theories available on how conflicts of an Indo-Pak nature may be resolved? If not, can a theory be attempted?

The continuing conflict between India and Pakistan can be seen through the ripeness model; mutually hurting stalemate (MHS), imminent catastrophe and entrapment models. Ripeness posits a realization to seek a way out at the time when parties feel hurting stalemate mutually. There have been at least four cases in which India and Pakistan realized that the ripe moment had arrived—the Tashkent Agreement 1966, Simla Agreement 1972, Lahore Declaration 1999 and Agra Summit 2001. Measures were taken during these efforts after calculating costs and benefits by India and Pakistan. The ongoing peace process between India and Pakistan that started in October 2003 may be considered as the fifth case, in which both countries have realized the need to resolve their bilateral conflict. In one case, during the Tashkent Agreement, a third party (the former Soviet Union) also identified ripeness of the situation but it could not bring about any long lasting or permanent settlement to their conflict. Similarly, both countries also experienced problems of imminent catastrophes at least on four occasions—during the Brasstacks crisis of 1986–7, the nuclear crisis in 1990, Kargil War in 1999 and the border confrontation in 2002.

Clearly, there were moments of confrontation but also an understanding of the need for its resolution. What made India and Pakistan to continue with confrontation irrespective of identifying the existence of ripe moments to resolve them? What made them forge ahead with peace efforts but fail to reach a final solution?

One factor that could be identified for the failure of India and Pakistan to convert the ripe moments into a long standing peace process, eventually leading to the resolution of conflicts has been the differences in perceiving of ripeness. Both India and Pakistan perceived the ripe moments from different angles. Both countries regularly passed through a point when they momentarily agreed that the time may be right for negotiations. At the same time, both sides at regular intervals decided that the risk of moving forward is too great. Often, they believed that time was on their side, and delay would weaken the case of the other side or strengthen its own. To some degree, both sides also believed that the other would not compromise unless confronted by overwhelming force.[1]

Ripeness theory deals with this perceptual dimension, however it insufficiently focuses on the persistent phenomenon of negotiations and cost-benefit analysis. India and Pakistan perceived ripeness according to their own cost-benefit analysis, based on their respective national interests. It also covered their domestic constituencies and interests. In a broader spectrum, it entails three elements; intra-party conflict behaviour, domestic conviction or consent, entrapment model. The first two are interlinked with each other. Every society shelters different schools of thought, comprising moderates, extremists, chauvinists and jingoists, who have diverse opinions and interests. In this context, both India

[1] Stephen P. Cohen, 'India, Pakistan and Kashmir', *Journal of Strategic Studies*, vol. 25, no. 4, December 2002, p. 24.

and Pakistan also breed different shades of opinions and perceptions that share some contributions in the policymaking process. Intra-party conflict behaviour can be determined through influence of prominent political and religious ideologues. In the wake of the Lahore Declaration, which was discredited by the Kargil War in 1999, 'the Indian proponents of a conciliatory line towards Pakistan came under strong attack from both the opposition parties and more hawkish elements of the BJP itself.'[2]

It is evident that most ripe moments in history of Indo-Pak peace efforts were adversely affected by internal politics of both countries, especially by the rightist elements in both countries. The Jamaat-i-Islami performed a ritual cleaning act of the Minar-i-Pakistan following Vajpayee's visit to the monument, while the Shiv Sena used 'Ganga-jal' to purify Mahatma Gandhi's memorial at New Delhi after General Pervez Musharraf's visit.[3]

As profound mistrust surrounds Indo-Pak societies, external ripeness depends upon the internal conviction of their domestic politics. Relevant to this factor of internal elements, the deadlock can also become a useful card to play domestic politics. The leadership views such a situation as an opportunity to prolong and ensure its tenure in local administration/government. Sabur discusses this domestic dimension with reference to Indian nuclear tests in 1998. 'The nuclear test has been designed to cultivate public support for BJP with a view to ensuring the stability of a fragile coalition. Even if the coalition headed by BJP fails to survive, this would result in popular mandate in favour of BJP.'[4]

Similarly, an Indian analyst considers certain ruling regimes under Indian and Pakistani leadership as a contributing factor to the atmosphere of hatred and animosity between the two countries. 'Bellicosity from L.K. Advani and Madan Lal Khurana on the one hand and Gohar Ayub Khan on the other has gone down well with hoi polloi in their respective countries but it underlines the

[2] Cohen, 'India, Pakistan and Kashmir', p. 13.

[3] Amitava Kumar, 'The Enemy Within', *Herald*, August 2001, p. 73.

[4] A.K.M. Abdus Sabur, 'Indo-Pakistan Security Relationship and the Kargil Crisis', *BIIS Journal*, vol. 20, no. 3, 1999, p. 247.

visceral Hindu-Muslim mutual hatred, either congenital or as a consequence of personal suffering at Partition.'[5]

The Indo-Pak leadership, to some extent, are also entrapped in a winning mentality against each other. This entrapment model, in its essence, offers a fixed mentality of leadership towards the cause (conflict) and consequence (impasse). Leaders become trapped into a continued pursuit of 'victory', even after the costs seem (to an outsider) to have become unbearable.[6] Under this model, the leadership becomes enthralled by a deadlock that transforms into 'investment' (also ensures the future role of leadership inside the country). This situation of a victorious mental attitude of parties spoils the ripe moment and parties cannot exploit the opportunity to their own advantage in the true sense of the word.

I. IS KASHMIR RIPE TO RESOLVE? IS THE STATUS QUO MUTUALLY HURTING?

Have India and Pakistan reached the MHS on Kashmir? A cursory look at events in the last decade would reveal that India, Pakistan and even Kashmiris have reached the MHS stage, and that there is no way other than reaching an understanding at the political level. It is clear, that none of the parties involved in the conflict—India, Pakistan, Kashmiris and militants, can alter the status quo through military means. The status quo, on the other hand is also not acceptable, as it is hurting all the parties concerned.

First, India and Pakistan have failed to alter the status quo in Kashmir, irrespective of the different political and military strategies that they employed in recent years. Before the Islamabad Summit in January 2004, there have been more than thirty-five occasions, in which the Heads of State in India and Pakistan met on various occasions (see Appendix 1).

[5] S.K. Mehra, 'Kashmir Issue-I', *The Statesman*, 7 July 1998.

[6] Christopher Mitchell, 'Cutting Losses: Reflections on Appropriate Timing', ICAR Working Paper 9, January 1996, <http://www.ciaonet.org/wps/mic01/> p. 5.

Besides these meetings at the highest levels, there were at least twelve rounds of talks between 1989 and 1998 before the Lahore and Agra Summits. Neither the meeting at the Heads of State level nor at the Foreign Secretary level, could proceed further. All these attempts invariably broke down, due to the failure of both governments to reach an understanding on Kashmir. The dialogue at the Secretary level in 1998 and that of the Lahore process in 1999, in particular were crucial, as both of them took place in the post-nuclear tests period. The 1998 talks at the Secretary level began with a lot of promise; the joint statement issued by the Foreign Secretaries of India and Pakistan in September 1998 read:[7]

> At each round the Foreign Secretaries will hold separate meetings on (a) peace and security including CBMs and (b) Jammu and Kashmir and review the progress of the dialogue process. The Foreign Secretaries will commence the substantive dialogue with separate meetings on (a) peace and security including CBMs and (b) Jammu and Kashmir in Islamabad on 15-18 October, 1998. The remaining six subjects i.e., (c) Siachen, (d) Wullar Barrage/Tulbul Navigation Project, (e) Sir Creek, (f) Terrorism and Drug Trafficking, (g) Economic and Commercial Cooperation, and (h) Promotion of friendly exchanges in various fields, shall be taken up in substantive and separate meetings in New Delhi in the first half of November 1998.

Despite the failure of the talks at the Foreign Secretary level, the Prime Ministers of India and Pakistan in 1999 made yet another attempt to reach an understanding on all issues including Jammu & Kashmir. According to the Lahore declaration, both India and Pakistan:[8]

- shall intensify their efforts to resolve all issues, including the issue of Jammu & Kashmir.
- shall refrain from intervention and interference in each other's internal affairs.
- shall intensify their composite and integrated dialogue process for an early and positive outcome of the agreed bilateral agenda.

[7] See the text of the joint statement made by the Foreign Secretaries of India and Pakistan, *The Hindu*, 25 September 1998.

[8] See the text of Lahore Declaration signed between the Prime Ministers of India and Pakistan on 21 February 1999.

- shall take immediate steps for reducing the risk of accidental or unauthorised use of nuclear weapons and discuss concepts and doctrines with a view to elaborating measures for confidence building in the nuclear and conventional fields, aimed at prevention of conflict.
- reaffirm their commitment to the goals and objectives of SAARC and to concert their efforts towards the realisation of the SAARC vision for the year 2000 and beyond with a view to promoting the welfare of the peoples of South Asia and to improve their quality of life through accelerated economic growth, social progress and cultural development.
- reaffirm their condemnation of terrorism in all its forms and manifestations and their determination to combat this menace.
- shall promote and protect all human rights and fundamental freedoms.

Besides the open diplomacy between the two countries, unknown to the outside world, including their foreign offices, the two Prime Ministers were also engaged in secret negotiations through their trusted emissaries. There were at least six rounds of talks between R.K. Mishra and Niaz Naik, who were widely believed to be the emissaries of Vajpayee and Nawaz Sharif respectively, before the conflict in Kargil shattered the calm. The first round took place between R.K. Mishra and Anwar Zahid during 3 and 4 March 1999 in Islamabad. Niaz Naik replaced Zahid, after the latter's untimely death and met Mishra in Islamabad on 20 March. A third round of talks between the two took place in New Delhi between 27 March and 1 April 1999. The fourth, fifth and sixth rounds took place in Islamabad on 12 April, 21 April and 17 May in Islamabad.[9]

Unfortunately, none of these processes could be sustained over a period, so that a peace process could be firmly established towards the final resolution of the bilateral conflicts, especially that of Kashmir.

[9] See Robert G. Wirsing, *Kashmir in the Shadow of War: Regional Rivalries in a Nuclear Age*, Armonk, NY: M.E. Sharpe, 2003, pp. 25–33.

II. A PAINFUL MILITARY DEADLOCK FROM KARGIL CONFLICT TO BORDER CONFRONTATION

Besides the political approach, both governments intermittently also attempted a military approach to alter the status quo in Jammu & Kashmir. The Kargil conflict, theories of limited war and pre-emptive strikes and the border confrontation in 2002—all were reflections of the attempt to alter the status quo in Jammu & Kashmir, militarily.

The Kargil conflict was seen by India as a three-phased plan by Pakistan. 'During the first phase, which is the boldest, Islamabad is seeking separation of the Kashmir valley from Ladakh. Simultaneously, it is making a concerted effort to entrench itself along the fulcrum of Chorbatla and Turtuk, north-east of Kargil. In the second phase, it has visualized sending in troops through the Chorbatla pass, north-east of river Indus. From here its forces could begin a thrust through the 'funnel' of Turtuk along the Shyok river to Khalsar where it meets the Nubra river. India's hold over Siachen would then become untenable. In the third and final stage, Pakistan would seek to consolidate itself and completely delink Ladakh from the rest of India incrementally.'[10] India believed that by cutting the NH-1A, Pakistan would interdict the Indian supply lines to its troops in Siachen, thus reducing its bargaining position.[11] India also believed that Pakistan's second aim was to 'give a fillip to militancy in Jammu and Kashmir by military action designed to weaken the counter-insurgency grid by drawing away troops from the Valley to Kargil. It would also give a boost to the morale of the militants in the Valley.'[12]

It was also believed in India that three factors figured in Pakistan's Kargil adventure—the internal situation in Kashmir which was improving slowly but steadily; general international response to Kashmir; and implications of any improved Indo-Pak relations

[10] Atul Aneja, 'Pakistan had three-phased plan?' *The Hindu*, 23 June 1999.

[11] J.N. Dixit, 'Invasion of Kargil', *Hindustan Times*, 23 June 1999.

[12] Kargil Review Committee Report, *From Surprise to Reckoning*, New Delhi: Sage Publications, 2000.

on Kashmir.[13] Shaukat Qadir's article on Pakistan's perception, which is widely considered as the only independent study on Kargil from the Pakistani side, also presented the same view. Accordingly, towards the end of 1998, the military leadership infused upon Nawaz Sharif that 'the freedom struggle in Kashmir needed a fillip, which could be provided by an incursion into these temporarily unoccupied territories' in the Kargil area.[14]

According to Shaukat Qadir, the political and military objectives of Pakistan's Kargil policy were as follows:

> The political aim underpinning the operation was 'to seek a just and permanent solution to the Kashmir issue in accordance with the wishes of the people of Kashmir'. However the military aim that preceded the political aim was to create a military threat that could be viewed as capable of leading to a military solution, so as to force India to the negotiating table from a position of weakness.[15]

However there are others who view Kargil in the larger Kashmir dispute context. According to them, Kargil was no different than any other border clash. They compare it to Siachen. It was a pre-emptive defensive move. It was also reported that the Indian forces were preparing for an operation in the area. According to Shireen Mazari:

> As the intelligence assessments about the suspicious movements of the Indian military in the late 1998-early 1999 period started looking more credible, the high command of the Pakistan Army asked FCNA to evolve a plan to deny the Indians any adventurism/incursions along the LoC, given Pakistan's historical experience on this account, especially on the lines of what happened in Siachen.[16]

[13] Suba Chandran, 'Why Kargil: Pakistan's Objectives and Motivations', in Maj. Gen. Ashok Krishna and P.R. Chari, eds., *Kargil: The Tables Turned*, New Delhi: Manohar, 2001, p. 33.

[14] Shaukat Qadir, 'An Analysis of the Kargil Conflict', *RUSI Journal*, April 2002, p. 26. Qadir also says that 'the military leadership had not presented a complete analysis of the scale of operation or its possible outcome, nor had they set out its political aim and how it would be achieved.'

[15] Qadir, 'An Analysis of the Kargil Conflict', p. 27.

[16] Shireen Mazari, *The Kargil Conflict 1999: Separating Fact from Fiction*, Islamabad: ISSI, 2003, p. 42.

The primary objective of Pakistan's Kargil adventure seems to be based on altering the status quo in Kashmir. Following the Kargil conflict, there was a serious attempt from a section in the Indian strategic community to alter the status quo in India's favour through a limited war and/or pre-emptive strikes. The main belief from the Indian side was that a limited war could be fought with Pakistan under the nuclear umbrella. George Fernandes, the then Indian Defence Minister, one of the pioneers of limited war with Pakistan stated that nuclear weapons 'can deter only the use of nuclear weapons, but not all and any war' and under the nuclear shadow, a 'conventional war remained feasible though with definite limitations if escalation across the nuclear threshold was to be avoided.'[17]

For the proponents of a limited war in India, the Kargil War is an example of an Indo-Pak limited war, as 'nuclear weapons did not make war obsolete. They simply impose another dimension of the way warfare could be conducted. The Kargil War was therefore handled within this perspective with obvious results.'[18] Jasjit Singh argues 'nuclear weapons have limited the aim, scope and extent of war among states that possess such capabilities because of the tremendously destructive potential of such weapons.'[19] India's belief is that 'since the onset of nuclearization has rendered "total war" unthinkable, "limited war" must of necessity be central to the military input into decision making'.[20]

The 2002 border confrontation, though its immediate cause was a terrorist attack on the Indian Parliament on 13 December 2001, had an underlying assumption that India could wage a limited war with Pakistan, so as to prevent the latter from supporting the separatist movement in the Indian Kashmir. According to Pakistani perspectives, the 2002 confrontation was an Indian military attempt to change the status quo in India's favour

[17] 'Fernandes Unveils "Limited War" Doctrine', *The Hindu*, 25 January 2000.

[18] George Fernandes, 'The Dynamics of Limited War', <http://www.stratmag.com/issueOct-15/page07.htm>

[19] Jasjit Singh, 'Dynamics of Limited War', *Strategic Analysis* (October 2000), p. 1206.

[20] Firdaus Ahmed, 'The Impetus Behind Limited War', *Peace and Conflict* 6, no. 2 (2003), p. 5.

by preventing Pakistan from aiding the separatist and militant movement.

The military build-up started after the 13 December 2001 attack on the Indian Parliament. New Delhi blamed Jaish-e-Muhammad, Lashkar-e-Taiba and Pakistan; while Islamabad categorically denied any involvement in the attack and offered a joint investigation. New Delhi persisted with its accusation.

The Indian Prime Minister announced on December 2001, that the attack on Parliament was an attack on 'the very existence and honour' of the nation and warned that all options were open.[21] C. Raja Mohan, a leading Indian commentator stated:

> The relations between India and Pakistan may have reached a decisive fork in the road—one path leading to war and the other to peace. If Pakistan does not quickly respond to the démarche delivered by India last week to shut down the operations of the terrorist organisations on its soil, India would be compelled to use force against it. A Pakistani retaliation would lead to escalation and a military confrontation. However, if Pakistan does crack down on Jaish-e-Muhammad and Lashkar-e-Taiba, a full-fledged peace processs could soon begin between India and Pakistan. If Pakistan curbs cross-border terrorism, India might be willing to initiate a full-fledged negotiation with Islamabad on all outstanding issues—including on Jammu & Kashmir and nuclear confidence-building measures. As India and Pakistan teeter between war and peace, the ball is in Gen. Pervez Musharraf's court.[22]

While a section inside India and Pakistan wanted that diplomacy should be given preference over of war,[23] some of them even suggested that war was not an option.[24] However, India be-

[21] 'All Options are Open: PM', *The Hindu*, 20 December 2001.

[22] C. Raja Mohan, 'Between War and Peace', *The Hindu*, 20 December 2001.

[23] Hussain Huqqani, 'India Should Make Diplomacy, Not War', *The Indian Express*, 20 December 2001; Praful Bidwai, 'Why War is no Option', *Hindustan Times*, 20 December 2001.

[24] According to a retired Indian General, 'Despite the mood for revenge, it is clear the military can't do much on the ground and in the air at present that will impress Gen Pervez Musharraf. India will have immense difficulty justifying war against terrorism outside J&K across the international border. Surgical air strikes across LoC in PoK are the only available option. Their utility in moulding Pakistan

gan mobilizing its troops; Pakistan followed suit. By 20 December 2001, the Indian Army started moving its strike formations including tanks and heavy artillery towards the border.[25] The border skirmishes began by the last week of December 2001 and the Indian defence minister announced that Indian missile systems were also 'in position'.[26] He stated in an interview that 'We Could Take a Strike and Survive, Pakistan Won't.'[27] Though Indian strategists were convinced that nuclear war was not a possibility, it was rather seen as an effort to reinforce the possibility of limited conventional war.[28] The Indian security forces even started laying landmines along the border.[29]

Using the military build-up, a section inside India wanted to bargain hard with Pakistan. According to them India failed to convert the military victory in 1971 into a political victory, by resolving the Kashmir conflict once and forever.[30]

---

behaviour is questionable, leave alone conflict escalation by Pakistan Air Force counteraction. Having occupied the moral and diplomatic high ground in Kargil by not crossing the LoC, it is debatable if aggression will be worthwhile now. Nations go to war when they are certain of a certain cost-benefit ratio.' See Ashok K. Mehta, 'Shifting Policies Deter Military Resolve', *The Pioneer*, 4 January 2002.

[25] 'Strike Forces Moved Closer to the Border', *The Hindu*, 21 December 2001.

[26] 'India's missile system "in position": Fernandes', *The Hindu*, 27 December 2001. This statement was given after the appearance of media reports in Indian newspapers that Pakistan had moved its missiles closer to the border. For details see *The Hindu*, 26 December 2001.

[27] 'We Could Take a Strike and Survive, Pakistan Won't: Fernandes', *Hindustan Times*, 30 December 2001.

[28] For example, K. Subrahmanyam wrote 'India is militarily stronger of the two antagonists. India has also pledged a no first use policy in respect of nuclear weapons. Invariably, all analysts predicting use of nuclear weapons in the Indo-Pakistan conflicts talk about a Pakistan, facing a disastrous defeat, being forced to resort to nuclear weapons. For reasons explained above, that situation is unlikely to arise. Secondly, the Indian armed forces are sensitive to tolerance limits of Pakistan and are not likely to force it into a situation when it would have to consider the use of nuclear weapons. Above all, the presence of US fleet in the Arabian Sea is the guarantor that nuclear weapons would not be used by Pakistan.' K. Subrahmanyam, 'Indo-Pak Nuclear Conflict Unlikely', *The Times of India*, 2 January 2002.

[29] 'Army, BSF Lay Mines along the LoC', *The Hindu*, 4 January 2002.

[30] According to a commentator, 'India's biggest defence and foreign policy blunder

Whatever be the initial efforts, India realized later that war was not an option. War with Pakistan would not bring any economic, political and strategic dividends. According to a retired Indian General:

> Despite the mood for revenge, it is clear the military can't do much on the ground and in the air at present that will impress Gen Pervez Musharraf. India will have immense difficulty justifying war against terrorism outside J&K across the international border. Surgical air strikes across LoC in PoK are the only available option. Their utility in moulding Pakistan behaviour is questionable, leave alone conflict escalation by Pakistan Air Force counteraction. Having occupied the moral and diplomatic high ground in Kargil by not crossing the LoC, it is debatable if aggression will be worthwhile now. Nations go to war when they are certain of a certain cost-benefit ratio.[31]

Rammanohar Reddy, commenting on the economic aspect, wrote:

> The implications of a war, however brief it may turn out to be, on two of the world's poorest economies should be self-evident. For India, first, there is the financial burden on the Central Government which has to meet the direct costs of the conflict. Second, there is the cost of displacement and disruption in the areas where the conflict will take place—both are likely to be considerable. And, third, there are the medium and even long—term costs the economy will experience in the form of lower economic growth. As against this the only benefit—if there can be such a thing in war—is that presumed to flow from better use of unutilised capacities in the economy.[32]

---

was committed by Mrs Indira Gandhi after the 1971 Bangladesh War. India had around 93,000 West Pakistani prisoners of war and we should have used them to settle the unresolved Kashmir dispute, by making their release conditional on Islamabad recognising the Line of Control as an international border. Instead of doing this, Mrs Gandhi returned the prisoners without seeking the slightest concessions on Kashmir.' Arvind Kala, 'Because Mrs G didn't Bargain', *The Indian Express*, 7 January 2002.

[31] See Ashok K. Mehta, 'Shifting Policies Deter Military Resolve', *The Pioneer*, 4 January 2002.

[32] C. Rammanohar Reddy, 'The Cost of War', *The Hindu*, 5 January 2002.

The then Indian Defence Minister, George Fernandes while addressing the Indian Parliament in May 2003 stated that 1,874 Indian soldiers lost their lives during this troop mobilization. The financial cost of this mobilization being well above Rs. 8,000 crore. According to a Pakistani analyst, due to the flight ban during the stand-off imposed by the Indian side, Indian flights to Kabul took a whole day to reach their destination and the flying time of Air India flights on major routes to Gulf, Europe and the US increased by at least an hour costing the already loss making Air India almost Rs. 100 crore on fuel charges only. A Pakistani scholar, referring to *The Tribune* stated that a ban on the Samjhauta Express train cost the Indian exchequer over Rs. 100 crore in one year; Rs. 25 crore was lost due to the discontinuation of train cargo services and another Rs. 48 crore was lost on account of the passenger ticket charges.[33]

The January 12 speech of General Musharraf reduced the threat of war.[34] A section inside India even saw it as a historic opportunity to resolve the Kashmir conflict.[35] An Indian Ministry of External Affairs note mentioned:

[33] Muhammad Irshad, 'Vajpayee's Hand of Friendship', *Defence Journal*, Karachi, June 2003 <http://www.defencejournal.com/2003/june/vajpayeehandoffriendship.htm>

[34] Gen Musharraf's January 12 speech was generally seen inside India as a positive development, though a section believed that he wilted under Indian military pressure. See Editorial, 'A Positive Gesture from Pakistan', *The Hindu*, 14 January 2002; Brahma Chellaney, 'India puts Musharraf in his Place', *Hindustan Times*, 14 January 2002.

[35] According to C. Raja Mohan, a leading commentator and a member of India's National Security Advisory Board, 'As India and Pakistan stare down the abyss of nuclear confrontation, there may be a historic opportunity at hand to move decisively towards a final resolution of the long-standing dispute over Jammu and Kashmir. If the international community succeeds in persuading the Pakistan President, Pervez Musharraf, to discard the instrument of cross-border terrorism with which Islamabad has bled India for nearly two decades, the confrontation could be de-escalated. And if Pakistan follows up with actions on the ground to curb terrorist activity on its soil, India must be ready to launch a serious political process that will explore an early and final solution to the Kashmir dispute.' See C. Raja Mohan, 'The Time is Now', *The Hindu*, 13 January 2002.

We welcome the now declared commitment of the government of Pakistan not to support or permit any more the use of its territory for terrorism anywhere in the world, including in the Indian state of Jammu and Kashmir. The commitment must extend to the use of all territories under Pakistan's control today. We would assess the effectiveness of the commitment only by the concrete action taken. Consequently, we expect Pakistan to cooperate with India in stopping all infiltration across the international border and the Line of Control (in Kashmir).[36]

If the Kargil confrontation could not alter the status quo for Pakistan, the border confrontation of 2002 could not do the same for India. Clearly, there is no military option, either for India or for Pakistan. Though the status quo could not be altered in military terms, both the countries are also aware that the status quo is hurting.

III. THE VALLEY
FESTERING WOUNDS, AND HEALING TOUCH

Despite the two elections for the state legislative assembly in the recent past and many other internal dialogues, India is yet to reach an agreement at the New Delhi-Srinagar level. Since the onset of militancy, the first elections for the state legislative assembly of Jammu & Kashmir took place in 1996. India believed that militancy had considerably declined by 1998; and normalcy was returning to the Valley, which could be seen from the fact that tourism was picking up in the Valley.[37] However, the National Conference, which formed the government failed to provide better governance; worse it became a 'profile of misgovernance'.[38]

If the State Government failed to provide good governance, the Union Government failed to make use of the changed atmosphere by initiating any serious discussion with the State Govern-

[36] See full text of statement issued by the Ministry of External Affairs in *The Times of India*, 14 January 2002.

[37] Elisa Patnaik, 'Tourism Slowly Picking up in Kashmir', *The Asian Age*, 13 September 1998. This view is not shared by both the researchers.

[38] Amitabh Mattoo, 'The Valley is Elsewhere', *The Indian Express*, 6 January 2000.

ment of Jammu & Kashmir. While a section inside the Kashmir Valley has been demanding total independence, others are demanding more autonomy for the State vis-à-vis the Union Government.[39] It is also to be noted that the majority in Jammu and Ladakh regions are against autonomy, as Ladakh wanted to become an Union Territory, while Jammu a state of the Indian Union.

Worse, when the National Conference government passed an autonomy resolution in the Jammu & Kashmir state legislative assembly, the Union Government rejected it without even discussing it in Parliament. During the same period, another initiative showed promise of bringing peace to Kashmir, but failed to sustain. The Hizbul Mujahideen, consisting mostly of Kashmiri militants announced a ceasefire in July 2000. The Union Government welcomed the ceasefire and initiated a dialogue with Majid Dar, the local Hizbul Mujahideen leader, who announced the ceasefire.[40] However, neither the Union Government nor the Hizbul Mujahideen could sustain the ceasefire, due to various reasons. First, the internal differences within the Hizbul Mujahideen, especially between Syed Salahuddin and Majid Dar. According to Indian perceptions, while Majid Dar wanted to pursue an independent policy, Syed Salahuddin was considered close to the Inter-Services Intelligence (ISI). The divide became apparent in the later years, in terms of Majid Dar and his associates getting expelled and subsequently assassinated, allegedly by the Salahuddin group.[41] Second, Salahuddin insisted on a tri-

[39] The separatists are led by the Hurriyat Conference, whereas the rest of the community in Jammu & Kashmir are represented by various political parties including the National Conference, Peoples Democratic Party and the Congress.

[40] See 'Centre Invites J&K Militants for talks', *The Hindu*, 29 July 2000; 'PM Hails Ceasefire Offer', *The Hindu*, 26 July 2000; 'Security Forces Told not to Jeopardize Ceasefire', *The Hindu*, 27 July 2000; 'Positive Development: Hizbul', *The Hindu*, 30 July 2000.

[41] For the divide inside the Hizbul see Praveen Swami, 'Fissures in the Hizb', *Frontline*, 26 April–9 May 2003; Praveen Swami, 'A Ceasefire in Kashmir', *Frontline*, 5–18 August 2000.

lateral dialogue involving Pakistan and announced a deadline for India doing so.[42] Third, India refused to accept any preconditions for a dialogue with the Hizbul Mujahideen which resulted in the dialogue failing to take off.[43]

In 2001 and 2002, India undertook two major initiatives towards Kashmir. First was an internal ceasefire, followed by the appointment of K.C. Pant and later N.N. Vohra as the government's chief interlocutors. The 2002 elections witnessed the Peoples Democratic Party (PDP) led by Mufti Mohammad Sayeed forming the coalition government along with the Congress and other parties. The elections were relatively fair and free, as compared to the earlier ones, though there were reports of coercion. For example, the Coalition of Civil Society observed 350 polling booths in fifty-six constituencies of Kashmir Valley and Doda district and concluded that 'the elections to the J&K assembly were flawed both in conception as well as conduct'.[44] The report looked into the larger dimensions of the entire electoral process and not just the elections. For example, the focus of the report included the deployment of security forces, extraordinary powers given to the security forces, non-revision of electoral rolls, denial of fundamental rights and civil liberties and the coercion by both the security forces and militants. Another independent report organized by the Institute of Social Sciences, New Delhi, which sent a forty-seven member study team to 450 polling stations in sixty-five constituencies concluded that the 'elections in Jammu and Kashmir which were held in four phases were fair. But it was

[42] 'Salahuddin sets August 8 Deadline for Tripartite Talks', *The Hindu*, 4 August 2000.

[43] 'No Role for Pakistan: PM', *The Hindu*, 7 August 2000.

[44] For the summary of the findings of the Independent Election Observer Team Report of the Coalition of Civil Society, see 'Kashmir Assembly Election: How Free and Fair?', *Economic and Political Weekly*, 11 January 2003, pp.101–5. For Pakistani perspective on these elections see, Shaheen Akhtar, 'IHK State Assembly Elections 2002', *Regional Studies*, vol. XXII, no. 2, Spring 2003, pp. 33–43 and *Regional Studies*, vol. XXII, no. 3, Summer 2003, pp. 71–135.

not necessarily free, particularly for those who have seen and lived with violence for the last 12 years'.[45]

Most of the population in Kashmir Valley, outside Srinagar, is dissatisfied with everything that has been happening for the last fifteen years. They prefer a peaceful life, with dignity and honour, with no violence either from the militants or security forces.[46] Many are aware that neither India nor Pakistan are going to agree to an independent Kashmir. One shopkeeper in Sopore commented, 'Indians have killed us; Pakistanis have killed us; Militants have killed us. The National Conference took our souls; the Hurriyat our children. No one speaks for us and we have no voice.'[47] A retired government official in Handwara summed up the feeling in the Valley, interpreting *The Gita*, 'whatever has happened, happened for bad; whatever is happening, is happening for bad; and whatever would happen, would happen for bad.'[48]

Despite the elections to the state legislative assembly and the formation of a new government led by the PDP, peace is yet to reach Kashmir. Mufti Mohammad Sayeed's 'healing touch' policy is yet to materialize at the ground level. Not many Kashmiris share Sayeed's enthusiasm over his 'healing touch'.[49] An account of militant attacks since October 2002 elections would reveal, that normalcy is yet to be restored (see Appendix III).

[45] For the findings of the ISS study see 'Jammu and Kashmir Assembly Elections 2002: Under the Shadow of Fear,' *Economic and Political Weekly*, 26 October 2002, pp. 4357–60. For a Pakistani perspective on these elections see, Shaheen Akhtar, 'IHK State Assembly Elections 2002', *Regional Studies*, vol. XXII, no. 2, Spring 2003, pp. 33–43 and *Regional Studies*, vol. XXII, no. 3, Summer 2003, pp. 71–135.

[46] Personal observations during the field trips conducted by one of the researchers on the Indian side of Jammu & Kashmir.

[47] Interviews during the field trips conducted by one of the researchers on the Indian side of Jammu & Kashmir.

[48] Interviews during the field trips conducted by one of the researchers on the Indian side of Jammu & Kashmir.

[49] See Mehraj Hajni and Ravinderjit Kaur, 'Mufti Government: Promises and Performances', *Peace and Conflict*, 7, no. 3, March 2004, pp. 21–2; Amin Masoodi, 'Mufti Government and the Healing Touch', <http://www.ipcs.org/Kashmir_articles2.jsp?action=showView&kValue=1135&issue=1012&status=article& mod=a>

All the three state actors—the Government of India, the Government of Pakistan and the Government of Jammu & Kashmir are in a situation where the status quo is hurting, though at a different level and intensity yet they all are aware, that there is no military option to resolve the conflict.

IV. SEPARATISTS AND MILITANTS

Besides the three major state actors, there are two non-state actors—the separatists led by the Hurriyat and the militants led by the Hizbul Mujahideen, Lashkar-e-Taiba (LeT) and Jaish-e-Muhammad. The Hurriyat has been under severe criticism and is facing a series of controversies. The Hurriyat has always been a highly divided organization, with the recent vertical split only adding to the problem. While one faction in the past had agreed to initiate a dialogue with the Union Government, the other led by Syed Ali Shah Geelani has rejected any such process.

The Hurriyat, with twenty-six parties and groups, has always been a divided house.[50] Worse, there is no road map for what is to be achieved.[51] What started the controversy during the recent period was the Hurriyat's official response to the 2002 state elections. While the faction led by Geelani wanted to undertake a campaign to boycott elections, the other faction led by the moderates was satisfied with the Hurriyat rejecting all pressure to participate in the elections. Geelani wanted strict action against the People's Conference, a component of the Hurriyat, for its rebels taking part in the 2002 elections.[52] While Geelani maintained that the rebel People's Conference members who took part in the elections had the support of its leadership, Sajjad Lone maintained that the rebels had been expelled and had no connections with them.[53] Sajjad Lone earlier maintained that Geelani

[50] In India the Hurriyat is primarily perceived to be Pakistan's proxy; In Pakistan it is considered to be the real representatives of the people of Kashmir.

[51] 'No Road Map on Kashmir: Malik', *Greater Kashmir,* 18 June 2003.

[52] 'Hawk Geelani tells Hurriyat: 'Take Harder Line or I Will Fly Away', *The Indian Express*, 5 July 2003.

[53] See Suba Chandran, 'All Parties Hurriyat Confusion: Implications of an Exit', http://www.ipcs.org/ipcs/issueIndex2.jsp?action=showView&kValue=

was responsible for the assassination of his father Abdul Ghani Lone and the latter even considered Geelani as an Indian agent.[54]

The July 2003 elections to the Hurriyat chairmanship, which resulted in Abbas Ansari being elected, only increased the divide within the Hurriyat. Geelani called the elections unconstitutional and refused to accept Ansari as the new chairman.[55] Besides, there was a struggle inside the Jamaat-e-Islami, Geelani's parent party, which is also a constituent of the Hurriyat.[56] Geelani wanted his own supporter to be elected as the next Jamaat chief in which effort he failed, as the organization elected Syed Nazir Ahmad Kashani, considered to be a moderate leader. Finally, the Hurriyat split vertically when a section close to Geelani formed a new faction.[57]

The militant organizations are also under tremendous pressure from both sides of the Line of Control (LoC). The Hizbul Mujahideen has also been facing splits, while the other two organizations—LeT and the Jaish are banned even in Pakistan. The split inside the Hizbul Mujahideen was visible after the announcement of the ceasefire of June 2000. Two groups emerged inside the Hizbul led by Syed Salahuddin and Abdul Majid Dar. The group led by Abdul Majid Dar considered Salahuddin as pursuing a pro-Pakistan policy, instead of a pro-Kashmir policy. Salahudin's group perceived Majid Dar as having been purchased by the Indian intelligence agencies.

The internal dissensions apart, the growing rapprochement between India and Pakistan has had a negative impact on the militant groups. There is open visible support for the dialogue

---

1106&issue=1012&status=article&mod=b ; Anirudh Suri, 'Recent Developments in All Party Hurriyat Conference – I', http://www.ipcs.org/ipcs/issueIndex2.jsp?action=showView&kValue=1143&issue=1012&status=article&mod=b

[54] 'Geelani is an Indian Agent, Claims Lone', *Hindustan Times*, 9 July 2003.

[55] 'Elections to Hurriyat Unconstitutional, Says Geelani', *The Hindu*, 20 July 2003.

[56] See 'Geelani defies Jamaat', *The Hindu*, 27 June 2003; 'Geelani Plans a New Front', *Hindustan Times*, 30 June 2003.

[57] Praveen Swami, 'Hurriyat Chairman Deposed, Claim Dissidents', *The Hindu*, 8 September 2003; 'Dissidents Want Geelani at Helm', *Daily Excelsior*, 9 September 2003.

inside the Valley and also inside Pakistan, which means less support to militancy. The Indian security forces have also improved their counter-insurgency operations. As a result, the militants are at the receiving end. More than 1,500 militants have been killed by the Indian security forces since 2003.[58] Besides, General Musharraf has taken a series of steps in the recent past towards curbing militant groups, which have affected them adversely.

V. FINAL TALLY
MANY SPOKESMEN, NO VOICES

All the actors, state and non-state, have attempted all means—political and military to change the status quo in their favour, but have failed to make any progress. The situation today in Kashmir closely represents Zartman's mutually hurting stalemate. The pain of deadlock and conflict over Kashmir is equally hurting and costly to all the parties involved in the conflict. They have paid huge costs in human, economic and defence terms.

According to an analyst, 'defence expenditures are a major burden mainly in India and Pakistan. They are particularly high in Pakistan—the country spends about 7 per cent of the GDP on defence compared to 3 per cent that of India.[59] Presently, India is a step ahead of Pakistan in military expenditure. India's military expenditure as percentage of GDP has grown from 2.10 in 1996 to 2.6 in 2002 and that of Pakistan during the same period has gone down from 5.10 to 4.50. However, as a percentage of central government expenditure, the military expenditure of India from 1996 to 2002 has hovered between 14.5–15 and that of Pakistan for the same period has come down from 24.0 to 21.20. What is more relevant in Pakistan's perceptions is that India has been consistently increasing their defence outlay and for the year 2003–4 the budget was raised by 14 per cent. Within two years of the

[58] See http://www.armyinkashmir.org/militant.html

[59] Akmal Siddiq, 'The Relevance of Economics and Environment in the South Asian Security', in Moonis Ahmar (ed.), *Paradigms of Conflict, Resolution in South Asia*, Dhaka: The University Press Limited, 2003, p. 89.

Kargil, India increased its defence spending by 50 per cent, which in real terms was equivalent to one and half times the total defence budget of Pakistan for the corresponding period (1999–2001).[60]

On the economic side, both countries are facing a crisis. Pakistan has a foreign debt of over thirty billion dollars, equaling half its GNP. More than half its budget is spent on defence or debt servicing, while less than 15 per cent goes to the social sector. Many Indians and Pakistanis are illiterate and deprived of the basic necessities of life. India's foreign debt has reached $ 100 billion and its budget deficit is 11 per cent of its GDP. Recently, India increased its defence spending by 28 percent.[61] They also incurred higher human costs during their military confrontations. During the Indo-Pak Wars of 1948 and 1965, 'more than 50,000 people died including civilians'.[62] Similarly, in the civil war in East Pakistan 1970–1, there were 'one million casualties', mostly civilians.[63] During the militancy in Kashmir since 1989 to 1998, 'over 30,000 civilians have died'.[64]

Leaving aside the painful political deadlock, the human and material casualties alone would make Kashmir a ripe issue for resolution. Clearly the costs are high, while benefits are less or none. If the deadlock continues it would only increase the costs. What is needed is that both India and Pakistan should realize the massive cost of the Kashmir conflict.

To conclude, all parties concerned have reached the mutually hurting stalemate stage. Is the situation then, ripe for resolution? The peace process that was initiated during the second half of 2003 and its sustenance in 2004 has made many believe that

[60] Lt. Gen. (Retd.) Talat Masood, 'Kashmir and Indo-Pak Conflict', *South Asian Journal*, no. 1, August–September 2003, p. 35.

[61] Rizwan Zeb, 'Peace Process and the News Media: A Closer Look at the Agra Summit', *Regional Studies*, vol. XXI, no. 2, Spring 2003, p. 60.

[62] Siddiq, 'The Relevance of Economics and Environment in the South Asian Security', p. 93.

[63] Ibid., p. 93.

[64] Ibid., p. 94. The figures represent Pakistani perspective, and is not shared by both the authors.

the time has arrived finally. Were Indo-Pak conflicts ripe to resolve in 2003, as they have reached a mutually hurting stalemate? Did the peace process of 2003–4 show any signs of ripeness? The next chapter would critically analyse the peace process to find some answers for the questions raised in this paper.

CHAPTER 3

The Peace Process in 2003–2004: Signs of Ripeness?

In October 2003, a new hope for peace emerged when New Delhi decided to review its year-long confrontational policy with Islamabad. It was a major breakthrough since India took the decision to cut all communication links and amass troops along the border after the terrorist attack on the Indian Parliament in December 2001.

Why did Vajpayee decide to change his government's policy regarding Pakistan? Was it the realization that the confrontational policy/military option had failed? Was it due to pressure from the international community led by the US? Was it due to internal pressure, with the ruling National Democratic Alliance (NDA) facing parliamentary elections in 2004? Was it due to Vajpayee's personal interest in resolving the Indo-Pak conflict, before he finally left the Prime Minister's Office? Or, was it simply because the time was ripe for the resolution of the Indo-Pak conflict?

How can one analyse Vajpayee's decision relating to the ripeness theory? It is possible that though at the ground level, the situation had reached the mutually hurting stalemate; the leadership would have failed to acknowledge or simply ignore it because ripeness itself is not a condition that the conflict would be resolved. If the ripe moment is not seized the conflict is likely to continue. In other words it is the realization and the seizure of the ripe moment that is the key to moving towards a resolution. The argument of economic costs by India was put forward as a factor by some analysts as a reason;[1] but many in India believe

[1] For details see Muhammad Irshad, 'Vajpayee's Hand of Friendship', *Defence Journal*, Karachi, June 2003, <http://www.defencejournal.com>

otherwise, as New Delhi was able and willing to bear those costs for national security. Some in India consider that it was nothing but the continuation of the then NDA government's 'strategic surprises'.[2] Some consider that it was an attempt by the Vajpayee government to find some 'diplomatic space.'[3]

The change in the Vajpayee government's policy could be analysed through the *enticing opportunity model*, according to which:

> . . . a ripe moment can occur when leaders see a much better alternative way of achieving their goals than 'slogging on' with continuing costly struggle. New options open up or are created which cost less and offer more gains more certainly than continued violence and mutual coercion. The emphasis is on new benefits rather than existing or anticipated costs, on rewards for adopting alternatives rather than on sacrifices that have to be compensated.[4]

The *enticing opportunity* model further states:

> For an opportunity to be enticing enough to persuade adversaries to think of moving towards a negotiated settlement, however, the prime determining condition appears to be that leaders and followers of both sides should be able to see major rewards on offer though the pursuit of some negotiated solution. For leaders, one of these rewards must usually be an anticipation that they will continue to play some further leadership role, and

[2] P.R. Chari, 'India's New Peace Initiative', http://www.ipcs.org/India_Pak_articles2.jsp?action=showView&kValue=1201& status=article&mod=a

According to Chari, 'India's nuclear tests in May 1998 shocked the world. Thereafter India made Pakistan's stoppage of cross-border terrorism a pre-condition to stall the normalisation of Indo-Pak relations just as Pakistan uses the Kashmir issue for this purpose. India relented suddenly, and set in motion its bus diplomacy, culminating in the Lahore Declaration of February 1999. The Kargil conflict intervened; but the consequent freeze in Indo-Pak relations was unfrozen by India's surprise invitation to President Musharraf for the Agra Summit in July 2000. Disappointment there led to another freeze in bilateral relations, worsened by the year-long border confrontation between December 2001 and October 2002, high rhetoric that no dialogue was possible without cross-border terrorism ceasing, and some 20 wanted criminals, provided asylum by Pakistan, being handed over.'

[3] See C. Raja Mohan, 'Vajpayee's Speech, a Bid to Regain Initiative', *The Hindu*, 19 April 2003.

[4] Christopher R. Mitchell, 'Cutting Losses: Reflection on Appropriate Timing', *ICAR Working Paper*, 9 January 1996, <http://www.cianet.org/wps/mic01>

what seems to have enticed a number of adversaries into a negotiated peace process in a variety of conflicts is a shared (if mutually contradictory, belief that, through a process involving negotiations followed by elections, they would win more cheaply the political power they were unable to obtain by coercive means.[5]

Perhaps the time was ripe to initiate a political process, because both countries cannot hurt the other more, without hurting themselves further. Non-cooperation and confrontation was not yielding any political gains vis-à-vis the other and also for its own internal political constituencies. The BJP government would have realized that the confrontationist posture was not providing any political gains either in India or with Pakistan.

The change in approach was visible since April 2003. Immediately before that, in February 2003, both countries acused the officials functioning in each other's embassies for pursuing activities against the other. India accused Jalil Abbas Jilani, Pakistan's Charge d'Affaires along with four other staff members of the Pakistan's High Commission in New Delhi for assisting separatists in Jammu & Kashmir and asked them to leave immediately.[6] Pakistan asked Sudhir Vyas, India's acting High Commissioner in Islamabad along with three others to leave Pakistan for pursuing activities not in accordance with their status.[7] Vajpayee, perceiving terrorism to be the main threat to India's unity and integrity stated in the Chief Minister's conference at New Delhi that 'the most disconcerting aspect of terrorism is that it is sponsored, supported and funded by Pakistan as a matter of its state policy.'[8] The BJP called for the closure of the Pakistan's High Commission in New Delhi.[9] Pakistan warned that ties may worsen further.[10]

In April 2003, there was a breakthrough, when Vajpayee of-

[5] Ibid.

[6] 'Pakistan envoy Asked to Leave India', *Hindustan Times*, 8 February 2003.

[7] 'Pakistan Directs Four Diplomats to Leave in 48 Hours', *The News*, 8 February 2003.

[8] 'Pak not Interested in Good Ties, Says PM', *The Hindu*, 9 February 2003.

[9] 'BJP Calls for Closure of Pakistan Mission', *The Hindu*, 9 February 2003.

[10] 'Ties may Worsen, says Islamabad', *Dawn*, 9 February 2003.

fered 'the hand of friendship' speaking from Srinagar.[11] Ultimately, in October 2003, India proposed twelve confidence building measures, including the resumption and extension of air and rail link; a new bus service between Srinagar in India and Muzaffarabad in Pakistan's administrated Kashmir, liberalization of the visa regime, and permitting people over sixty-five years of age to cross the border at Wagah on foot.[12]

Pakistan's foreign secretary, Riaz Khokhar, while addressing a press conference on 29 October, announced that Pakistan accepts all rational CBMs.[13] Islamabad reciprocated with its own set of CBMs. Islamabad offered to start an additional bus service from Lahore to Amritsar; revival of rail links; a hundred scholarships for Kashmiri students; free treatment of forty Indian patients in Pakistani hospitals; and a proposal for rehabilitation of Kashmir victims, etc.[14] Towards the end of 2003, there was another set of CBMs proposed by India which included transport links between Srinagar and Muzaffarabad; and Munabao (Rajasthan) and Khokrapar (Sindh).[15] These proposals kept increasing in 2004; according to a news report, between April 2003 and October 2004, there were nearly ninety-six CBMs proposed by both countries.[16]

BREAKTHROUGHS AND DEADLOCKS

What did India and Pakistan achieve since then in the next fourteen months?[17] What were the major achievements and failures? What were the reasons therefore? What were the stumbling blocks?

[11] 'PM Talks Pak, Peace and Prosperity in J&K', *The Times of India*, 18 April 2003.

[12] Amit Baruah, 'India Proposes a Dozen Steps to Break the Ice with Pak', *The Hindu*, 23 October 2003.

[13] Rizwan Zeb, 'Recent Indo-Pak Offers: Old Wine in New Bottle?', http://www.ipcs.org/newKashmirLevel2.jsp?action=showView&kValue=1223&subCatID=null&mod=null. For further details see *Dawn*, 30 October 2003, *The Nation*, 30 October 2003.

[14] Ibid.

[15] 'Pakistan Gets New Year Card Full of CBMs', *Hindustan Times*, 1 January 2004.

[16] '96 CBMs Exchanged by India, Pak since April 2003', *The Tribune*, 31 October 2004.

[17] This study covers the developments only upto December 2004.

Were the conditions during 2002–3 not adequate for the Indo-Pak conflicts to become ripe for resolution?

The progress in fourteen months could be broadly classified into achievements, deadlocks and failures. On the achievements side, both countries were able to initiate a structured dialogue, though how far they have been sustained and would sustain in 2005 remains to be seen. The first major achievement took place at Islamabad in January 2004 during the South Asian Association of Regional Cooperation (SAARC) Summit. Prior to the summit, despite repeated statements by India, observers believed that during the summit, both sides would be able to move ahead with the normalization process.[18]

Both leaders met during the SAARC Summit and managed to issue a joint statement. According to the joint statement, 'the resumption of the dialogue will lead to a peaceful settlement of all bilateral issues, including Kashmir, to the satisfaction of both sides'.[19] President Musharraf stated the meeting as a victory of moderates in India and Pakistan and that it was Vajpayee's vision and statesmanship which made it possible.[20] Colin Powell offered to use American good offices in India and Pakistan for favourable purposes.

According to a leading Pakistani analyst, in contrast with the post-war Tashkent and Simla Summits, the Islamabad Summit, and the Lahore Summit produced results. One of the primary results of the latter summits was the emergence of the Pakistan military leadership as the principal 'interlocutor on the Pakistani side, thereby reducing sabotage of the process from within'.[21] The 6 January breakthrough came about because of a number of reasons. Nasim Zahra lists five main reasons:[22] back-channel interaction; acknowledgement of ground realities on both sides;

[18] Rizwan Zeb, 'From War to Peace: Will it Last?', http://www.ipcs.org/newKashmirLevel2.jsp?action=showView&kValue=1303&subCatID=null&mod=null

[19] Ibid.

[20] Ibid.

[21] Nasim Zehra, 'Why Did It Work At Islamabad', *The News*, 8 January 2004 <http://www.jang.com.pk/news/jan2004-daily/08-01-2004/oped/01.htm>

[22] Ibid.

the personal factor; American and British encouragement; and keeping the decision to meet and to produce a joint statement 'under wraps'.

The two leaders also met in New York later. This meeting, details of which are still mostly secret, was termed by both as successful. The Indian Prime Minister termed the meeting as historic and a new beginning.[23] President Musharraf declared that the talks 'augured well for the future of Pakistan and India'.

Besides the Islamabad meeting, there were crucial meetings at the secretary and ministerial levels. The foreign secretaries of both countries met in September 2004 to review the process. Both sides agreed that the overall atmosphere has been positive and progress has been made on the eight subjects in the composite dialogue.[24] (Peace and security including CBMs, Jammu & Kashmir, Siachen, Sir Creek, Wullar Barrage/Tulbul Navigation Project, Terrorism and Drug Trafficking, Economic and Commercial Cooperation and Promotion of Friendly Exchanges.) The foreign ministers of both countries also met and reiterated the confidence that the composite dialogue will lead to a peaceful settlement of all issues.

According to a news report both agreed on the following:[25]

> Expert level meetings on conventional and nuclear CBMs, inter alia, to discuss the draft agreement on advance notification of missile tests; Meeting between railway authorities on the Munnabao-Khokharapar rail link; Bi-annual meeting between Indian Border Security Force (BSF) and Pakistani Rangers in October 2004; meeting between Narcotics Control Authorities, including for finalisation of an MoU in October/November 2004; meeting between the Indian Coast Guards and the Pakistani Maritime Security Agency in November 2004 to inter alia, discuss the Memorandum of understanding for establishing communication link with

[23] Tarun Basu, 'Manmohan Calls it "Historic Day" After Summit with Musharraf', *Indo-Asian News Service*, 24 September 2004 <http://in.news.yahoo.com/040924/43/2gcvi.html>

[24] Joint Press Statement on the meeting between Foreign Secretaries of India and Pakistan, 4 September 2004 <http://meaindia.nic.in>

[25] Text of Joint Statement issued at Indo-Pak Talks Conclusion, *Pakistan Times*, 5–6 September 2004 <http://www.pakistantimes.net/2004/09/09/top11.htm>

them; Establishment of a Committee of experts to consider issues related to trade; On Siachen, the outcome of the August 2004 meeting of Defence Secretaries would be implemented; Joint Survey of the boundary pillars in the horizontal segment (blue dotted line) of the International Boundary in the sir Creek area; Meeting on all issues related to commencement of a bus service between Srinagar and Muzaffarabad; Add a new category of Tourism visa in the visa regime between the two countries, and promote group tourism; Set up a mechanism to deal with the issue of civilian prisoners and fishermen, effectively and speedily; Further measures for facilitation of visits to religious shrines and upkeep of historical sites; and Enhanced interaction and exchanges among the respective Foreign Offices including study tours of young diplomats/probationers to each other's country.

The foreign secretaries met again in December 2004 during the two day 'evaluation of the peace process' meeting at Islamabad. India announced that senior citizens and children could avail of a visa at Atari. Shyam Saran, the Indian Foreign Secretary also announced Indian willingness to give visas to Pakistani students who would like to study in India and that twenty more children would be treated in Indian hospitals. On Kashmir, however India rejected the suggestion to include Kashmiris in the talks, claiming that Indians represent Kashmir. He further said that 'Pakistan must adhere to the commitment made in the statement by Pakistani President Pervez Musharraf and Indian Prime Minister Manmohan Singh of 6 January 2004 in the US regarding stopping cross-border terrorism'.[26] India also proposed reunion of divided Kashmir families at five different points on the LoC.[27] Pakistani foreign secretary, Riaz Khokhar, while talking to the media, categorically stated that 'we are clear about having implemented the assurances given in the January 6 joint statement. Nothing is happening across the LoC, but regrettably human rights violations have increased in Kashmir'.[28]

Besides the foreign secretaries, the foreign ministers of both

[26] 'Indian Visas to Elderly and Children at Atari', *Daily Times*, 28 December, 2004.

[27] 'India Suggests Reunions for Kashmiri Families', *Daily Times*, 29 December 2004.

[28] Ibid.

countries also held meetings. They met during the Asian Co-operation Dialogue (ACD) meeting in China in June 2004 and later during the eleventh annual meeting of the Association of South-East Asian Nations' Regional Forum (ARF) in Jakarta in July.[29] The meeting was termed as extremely successful by both sides. The Pakistani foreign minister also met the Indian Prime Minister and the Indian National Security Advisor. It was decided that the Pakistani President and the Indian Prime Minister will meet during the United Nations General Assembly (UNGA) session in New York, later in the month and that the two foreign ministers will meet in December to evaluate the progress made in the peace process.[30]

The second major achievement was the understanding between both sides to establish back-channel diplomacy. Both governments revitalized the back-channel interaction, when the process was stumbling, especially after the new government in India took over. There were reports stating that the back-channel diplomacy undertaken silently by Brajesh Mishra and Tariq Aziz, the trusted aides of Vajpayee and Musharraf respectively was crucial to the breakthrough during the SAARC Summit in January 2004.[31] Elections were held for the Indian Parliament at this crucial juncture and there was widespread expectation that the BJP-led alliance would be able to form the government again. The formation of government by the Congress I-led alliance was a surprise for many in India and outside. From Pakistan's perspective, there were reasons for being enthusiastic about the new Indian government led by Dr Manmohan Singh. At the governmental level, in Islamabad, there were no misapprehensions with the Congress and its allies in New Delhi. There was widespread optimism that the peace process would proceed further irrespective of the change

[29] See 'Natwar Singh-Kasuri Meeting "Productive"', *The Hindu*, 22 June 2004; 'India, Pakistan Agree to Sustain Dialogue Process' , *The Hindu*, 3 July 2004.

[30] Text of Joint Statement issued at Indo-Pak Talks Conclusion, *Pakistan Times*, 5-6 September 2004 <http://www.pakistantimes.net/2004/09/09/top11.htm>, also see *IPRI Fact File*, Islamabad Policy Research Institute, vol.VI, no. 10, October 2004, p. 77.

in government. The statements issued by the Congress leader, Sonia Gandhi that the peace process with Pakistan would go on added to this optimism. The then Prime Minister designate, Manmohan Singh also said that India would seek friendly relations with Pakistan. In response, Islamabad showed its readiness to work with the new Indian government.

However, this atmosphere of goodwill inside Pakistan suffered a blow when New Delhi postponed the expert-level discussion on nuclear CBMs. The new government in India wanted some time to consolidate; but this delay raised anxiety inside Pakistan. However, the general mood in Pakistan remained optimistic that this was an isolated event and the change of guard would have no adverse effect on the ongoing peace process. At the same time, there were few, raising concerns regarding the prospects of the process. According to them, in contrast to Vajpayee, who had a personal interest in the process as he wanted to go down in history as a peacemaker, the Congress leadership had no such personal involvement. They also pointed out that even though the former Prime Minister was in a position to deal with Pakistan, especially on the issue of Kashmir; ironically, he and this team would accuse Congress of a sellout if it tried to move ahead on the issue of Kashmir with Pakistan.

This viewpoint was further supported by statements coming out of New Delhi, such as 'the India-China model will be followed for dealing with Pakistan', 'LoC as IB', 'economic relations first, the rest later', especially J.N. Dixit's statement in which he ruled out any possibility of giving away even an inch of Indian administrated Kashmir's territory to Pakistan.'[32] It was at this juncture, that Tariq Aziz met J.N. Dixit at Amritsar,[33] reviving the peace process. The postponed expert level meeting on nuclear CBMs took place in earnest.

The following factors are significant in assuming that a silent diplomacy through trusted aides is a better option: the level of rhetoric; pressure from various internal actors; rigid postures and

[32] Rizwan Zeb, 'Can the Indo-Pak Peace Process be Saved?'

[33] Ibid.

mentalities amongst the various institutions engaged in dialogue; and vested interests in India and Pakistan. The R.K. Mishra—Niaz Naik channel between Vajpayee and Nawaz Sharif was proceeding in the right direction before hostilities broke out in Kargil. It is essential that the leadership at the highest levels both in India and Pakistan make use of this option, while other institutions are engaged in an open diplomacy.

The third major achievement was the rapid growth in traffic between both countries at the non-governmental level in terms of people-to-people level contacts. This took place at various stages from Track II to popular levels creating a tremendous impact in the psyche of the people about the other. One major effort at the track two level was the meeting between two groups led by M.K. Rasgotra and Niaz Naik in January 2004.[34] Another delegation led by the Act Now for Harmony and Democracy (ANHAD) and Action Aid undertook a week-long trip to Pakistan.[35] The international book fair in New Delhi witnessed more publishers from Pakistan and Indians took special interest in books from across the border.[36] A group of Pakistani scouts attended the SAARC camp held at Gulmarg in Kashmir Valley.[37]

More than these movements, what captured the minds of people both in India and Pakistan was the Indo-Pak cricket matches during March 2004, which witnessed Indian fans heading to Pakistan and the warm reception extended to them by the hosts. The interior ministry in Pakistan announced that it would provide visas to everyone who possessed valid match tickets.[38] Besides the cricket matches, another significant achievement at the popular level contacts were the visits of journalists from India and Pakistan to the two Kashmirs. Journalists from Pakistan

[34] See 'Indian Track II Team Arriving in Pak', *Hindustan Times*, 19 January 2004; 'Track II Diplomacy Back on Track', *The Nation*, 20 January 2004; 'Indo-Pak Track II Doves Moot 16 Points Peace Plan', *Hindustan Times*, 22 January 2004.

[35] 'Indian Team Arrives on Peace Mission', *Dawn*, 2 February 2004.

[36] 'Book Fair a Success Story for Pak Publishers', *The Tribune*, 20 February 2004.

[37] 'Pakistani Scouts attend SAARC Camp at Gulmarg', *The Hindu*, 6 July 2004.

[38] 'Pakistan Pledges 5750 Visas for the ODIs', *The Times of India*, 26 February 2004.

visited Kashmir in October 2004 and Indian journalists visited Pakistani Kashmir later.[39]

Deadlocks

While the breakthrough could be divided into three broad headings, the deadlock was primarily regarding the gas pipeline.

Pakistan has been willing to reach an agreement with India on providing pipelines through its territory from Iran and other Central Asian countries.[40] India has been hesitating to agree for three reasons—political, security and economic.

Political concerns have always been primary in reaching a decision on whether India should agree to gas pipelines passing through Pakistan. Sumitra Mahajan, Minister for State for Petroleum in a written statement made the political concerns clear: 'Keeping in view the present state of bilateral relationship with Pakistan, the government is not considering any proposal for onland natural gas pipeline transiting through Pakistan.'[41] Yashwant Sinha, the then Indian Foreign Minister also made a similar statement linking political relations with gas pipelines. He stated: 'If Pakistan can find within itself the strength and wisdom to change its current approach towards India, there are immense benefits that it can derive as a transit route for the movement of energy, goods and people'.[42]

One of the major security concerns has to do with India's vulnerability with regard to an overland pipeline. Fear is voiced that Pakistan could cut off supply, or else militants would do so starving India of its energy requirements. Those who emphasize

[39] See 'the following reports and articles for the impact created by the journalists' visits in India and Pakistan: 'Soften Borders, say Pakistani Scribes', *The Hindu*, 5 October 2004; 'A Remarkable Visit: Pakistani Scribes', *The Hindu*, 10 October 2004.

[40] See 'Help Offered to India on Gas Pipeline Project', *Dawn*, 14 July 2003; 'Pakistan Backs Iran-India Gas Pipeline', *The News*, 17 October 2003; 'Jamali Raises Gas Pipeline Issue', *The Hindu*, 7 January 2004.

[41] 'Pipeline via Pak not Acceptable: India', *The Times of India*, 29 July 2003.

[42] 'India Ready to Consider Gas Pipeline via Pakistan', *Dawn*, 3 January 2004.

on security concerns in India link it to reaching a broad political understanding resulting in peace. Ram Naik, former Minister for Petroleum commented: 'Peace is something which is necessary and a gas line is very explosive. . . Anyone can play with the pipeline.'[43]

Security analysts in India have however downplayed such threats. According to Jasjit Singh:

> An agreement to build a pipeline for transportation of natural gas would not be a bilateral issue between Pakistan and India. It would require the participation of the producer country, any other transit country (like Afghanistan), international financial institutions (like World Bank and Asian Development Bank who have indicated their interest in funding such projects), Pakistan and, of course, India. All these players would have to invest in the project and hence would have a stake in its continued efficiency. Pakistan's own investments would be adversely affected in case of supply disruption. Above all, there are international precedents, potentially binding legal arrangements and safeguards available to guard against supplies being cutoff.[44]

A number of Indian observers have argued that 'the gas pipeline contract could be made far more secure for India by building comprehensive provisions for supply of petroleum products and power to Pakistan. In other words, the contract could be structured in a manner that makes any disruption in supply expensive and strategically infeasible to Pakistan'.[45] Natwar Singh, India's external affairs minister is on record stating that India would consider gas pipelines via Pakistan provided the latter agree for international security guarantees.[46]

Besides the political and security concerns, economic factors has also played a crucial role in India's decisions on the pipeline through Pakistan. India prefers to enter into an agreement with

[43] 'India Rejects Proposal for Import of Gas via Pakistan', *Hindustan Times*, 12 December 2003.

[44] Jasjit Singh, 'Not Pipedreams', *The Indian Express*, 23 July 2003.

[45] R.K. Pachauri, 'An Indo-Pak Peace in the Pipeline?' *The Times of India*, 5 February 2004. Also see editorial, 'Peace this Pipeline', *The Indian Express*, 20 July 2004; and Inder Malhotra, 'Gas Pipelines via Pakistan', *The Tribune*, 22 July 2004.

[46] 'India may Consider Gas Pipeline via Pak', *The Indian Express*, 5 June 2004.

Pakistan on pipelines on a broader economic canvass.[47] This includes Pakistan providing India the Most Favoured Nation (MFN) status;[48] and transit rights to Iran, Afghanistan and other Central Asian countries.[49] Despite various meetings and discussion, the issue remain deadlocked.

Fourteen Months: A Tally

Since Vajpayee's third and apparently the last attempt, both sides are continuously engaged in a dialogue process; there have been both achievements, though not spectacular and deadlocks, which causes concern. The 'trust deficit' as phrased by General Musharraf remains significant in the dialogue process.[50] Already there have been criticisms that the present thaw between the two countries will not last.[51]

Would the peace process only achieve an absence of a continuous threat of war? Pakistan believes that in spite of visible actions being taken against the jehadis (cross-LoC terrorism issue), there have been no major or visible change in the human rights situation in Kashmir or towards the resolution of the issue (the larger Kashmir Issue). According to an analyst, '. . . two clear trends in the Indian approach can be discerned: One, to sustain the dialogue process while circumventing a substantive discussion on the resolution of the Kashmir issue. Two, to move towards cooperation in the fields of trade and economic cooperation as

[47] Natwar Singh, India's external affairs minister stated: 'We could recommend to Pakistan that we discuss the setting up of the pipeline from Panipat to Pakistan in the context of our discussions on the Iran-Pakistan-India gas pipeline since this would conform to the agreement by both sides to look at these issues in the larger context of expanding trade and economic relations between India and Pakistan'. See 'Full steam ahead on Iran gas via Pak', *The Indian Express*, 25 October 2004.

[48] 'Gas Pipeline Project Hinges on MFN Status to India', *The Hindu*, 11 January 2004.

[49] 'India Keen on Transit Rights as Part of Pipeline Deal', *The Hindu*, 13 October 2004.

[50] 'Indian Visas to Elderly and Children at Atari', *Daily Times*, 28 December 2004.

[51] For details see Stephen Philip Cohen, 'Testimony Before the Senate Foreign Relations Committee on India and Pakistan: Steps Towards Rapprochement', http://www.brookings.edu/dybdocroot/views/testimony/cohens/20040128.pdf

well as increasing people to people contact.[52] India believes that actions taken by Pakistan on controlling the terror machinery is not sufficient and is in a haste to reach an agreement on Kashmir, imposing its perceptions.

Pakistan perceives that peace between the two countries is not possible without the resolution of Kashmir issue. Pakistani President General Musharraf while answering a question during the India Today Conclave said:

> No leader in Pakistan can sideline the Kashmir issue. Now this is the reality and we cannot do it. If we think that we can go ahead on all confidence-building measures and forgot about Kashmir, not doable by any leader in Pakistan. We must understand this basic issue; I don't think we can move forward. Let me put it very bluntly. I don't think we can move forward on the confidence building measures. I don't think we can move forward on the economic interaction unless we move forward on resolution of all dispute including the Kashmir dispute.[53]

Though the Indian Government has been hesitant in openly agreeing, there is no doubt that a resolution of the Kashmir conflict is significant to the success of any peace processes between India and Pakistan. But how to resolve it and when? Should there be a timeframe? Which institutions are needed to reach a compromise and what procedures are to be pursued?

India and Pakistan need to look into these issues, which remain as stumbling blocks, irrespective of both countries realizing that the status quo is hurting and not acceptable. In terms of ripeness for the resolution of conflicts, something else is still needed. A middle ground needs to be found, so that both countries reach a compromise. In other words, the situation is apparently ripe, but needs some artificial assistance so that this ripe moment can be seized. The next chapter looks into ways such conditions could be created.

[52] Shireen Mazari, 'India's Peace Dilemma', *Strategic Studies*, vol. XXIV, no. 4, Winter 2004, p. 1.

[53] Interview of President General Pervez Musharraf to The India Today Conclave, 13 March 2004, http://www.infopak.gov.pk/President_Address/india_today_conclave.htm

CHAPTER 4

Indo-Pak Ripeness
Irritants and Inducements

The most dominant irritant in the Indo-Pak conflict is the identification of the core of their differences. Both India and Pakistan hold different views regarding their conflict, especially on what constitutes the core; to Pakistan it is Kashmir, whereas for India it is Pakistan's support for cross-border terrorism across the LoC. India has condemned Pakistan for interfering in India's internal affairs. Pakistan has however, consistently declared that despite its concern over the situation in Indian Kashmir it has not incited the uprising—it still insists on an UN supervised plebiscite to resolve the conflict. This appears to be the main irritant throughout the recent history of Indo-Pak peace efforts. The Agra Summit in 2001 ended without any documented declaration because both India and Pakistan failed to decide what constituted their core of the differences; Kashmir or cross-border terrorism.

Is Kashmir really a core issue? For Pakistan, four factors make Kashmir a core issue. At the national level, Pakistan terms Kashmir as a core issue because it believes in the historical orientation of the Kashmir conflict. On the basis of the two-nation theory, Kashmir (a Muslim majority state) should have acceded to Pakistan but it did not. Moreover, Pakistan and India have fought three major wars on Kashmir. Pakistan therefore cannot put Kashmir on the backburner. Second, at the regional level, Kashmir deserves to be a core issue because India alleges that Pakistan is supporting terrorism in Jammu & Kashmir.

Third, according to Pakistan, Kashmir is a core issue at the international level because it has gained international recognition as a conflict and nuclear flashpoint, threatens regional peace in particular and world peace in general. The Kashmir issue has been part of the international political system for the past four decades, it has been affected by the UN mediation processes and superpower politics. The Kashmir dispute was first internationalized in 1948, when India brought the issue to the UN Security Council after accusing Pakistan of sending armed infiltrators into Kashmir. Finally, according to Pakistan, most of the accords and agreements between India and Pakistan focused on Kashmir, especially the Tashkent Declaration 1966 and Simla Accord 1972. Among them, the Simla Accord would not have focused on Kashmir (if it was not a core issue) because it was signed in the backdrop of Indian interference in the East-Pakistan crisis of 1971. Hence, for Pakistan, Kashmir is a core issue.

India, till today has officially refused to accept Kashmir as the core issue. India wants to improve relations with Pakistan on the basis of other issues, especially trade and cultural exchanges including improvement of people-to-people contacts. India's perception is based on the belief that movement on non-Kashmir issues, would soften the hostile opinion vis-à-vis each other, leading to the creation of a better environment in which the Kashmir issue could be discussed. If India is to accept Pakistan's perception of Kashmir as the core issue, then it needs to be settled first, before other issues. Pakistan fears that once there is a movement in other fields, the Kashmir issue would subside and India may refuse to negotiate at a later stage.

The second irritant in creating a better atmosphere is that both India and Pakistan cultivate psychological approximations against each other. Stereotype and mirror images, ill will, suspicions, and paranoia lead them nowhere but to be engaged in continued hostility with each other. They bear the burden of history. Whenever dialogues took place, agreements were signed, both countries were caught up by mutual misgivings. After the Simla Agreement, disputes were to be resolved based on a set of guidelines that it provided to India and Pakistan. The Simla Agreement could never be implemented in letter and spirit due to the misgivings immediately after the treaty was signed. The nuclear test by India in 1974, Pakistan's role against Soviet troops in Afghanistan since 1979, the threat of an Indian attack on Kahuta, the Brasstacks and the 1990 nuclear crisis coupled with two militancies in Punjab and Kashmir never let both countries adhere to the spirit of the Simla Agreement.

I. CAN RIPENESS BE ARTIFICIALLY INDUCED? CREATING PRECONDITIONS TO INDO-PAK RIPENESS

It has been clearly established, that India and Pakistan, along with other actors including the militants and Kashmiris have reached the mutually hurting stalemate as defined by William Zartman. Why then, has MHS not paved the way for resolution? Does the MHS situation in the Indo-Pak context demand some facilitation? Does it need a stimulant? If yes, how can they be induced?

One of the main reasons why the MHS in Kashmir has not automatically created a ripe condition has been that the conflict between India and Pakistan is focused not only on Kashmir, though it has its roots in it. Siachen, Sir Creek and the Wullar Barrrage/ Tulbul Navigation Project are some of the other significant points of conflict between the two countries. Unfortunately, the human and economic costs of these flashpoints have not been given adequate attention either by the governments or the strategic community. As a result, public understanding including that of legislators on the social and economic costs of these points of discord is either minimal or non-existent. The political significance and the popular obsession with the Kashmir conflict on both sides of the border have subsumed the costs of the other contending factors. This has resulted in periodic and calculated upheavals in non-Kashmir conflicts, never providing an opportunity for them to reach the MHS stage. Probably, it may never reach the point of hurting all the parties involved. In that case, how to factor in these low profile points of contention which would never reach the MHS stage into a high profile and volatile conflict that has already reached the required stage?

Second, though both the countries have reached the MHS stage, there is no readymade alternative path that could be pursued. Unfortunately, the cost-benefit analysis of Indo-Pak antagonism in their totality, taking into account the probability of a future open conflict is yet to reach the people or their representatives. The presence of nuclear weapons along with problems of its safety, security and nuclear command has added an extra dimension to the existing fault times.

Given the enormity of Indo-Pak rivalry, it is not an easy task pushing them to realize and seize the ripe moment to eliminate their hostility. Irrespective of reaching the MHS, it is essential that certain preconditions are created in terms of facilitating both the countries. These preconditions for Indo-Pak ripeness could focus on the following aspects: structural, economic and political/ military.

II. INDO-PAK CONFLICTS AND ENGAGEMENTS STRUCTURING AND PRIORITIZING

First, it is essential that India and Pakistan create an overall conflict management structure with a timeframe towards reaching an understanding. More than reaching an agreement, it is imperative to initiate a process. Or, a series of processes on various dimensions of conflict. These structured processes should be both independent and integrated. They would be independent, in the sense, that each process would have its own timetable and structure and it would be integrated, in the sense that they would function in the same space.

Each of these processes should be clearly defined in terms of their focus and objectives. There were instances in the past, in which both countries, after establishing working groups, found it difficult to agree which group should focus on what issues. In one of the bilateral meetings in September 1998, Sartaj Aziz, Pakistan's foreign minister was quoted stating. 'There have been no successful parleys. Differences exist on which working group should take up what issue . . . When there are so many hitches at the initial stages, we wonder how the dialogue will proceed fruitfully.'[1]

It was decided in June 1997 at the Foreign Secretary level that both countries would 'address all outstanding issues of concern

[1] See 'No Breakthrough in Talks, says Pak', *The Hindu*, 2 September 1998.

to both sides including, inter alias: (a) Peace and security, including CBMs; (b) Jammu & Kashmir; (c) Siachen; (d) Wullar Barrage Project/Tulbul Navigation Project; (e) Sir Creek; (f) Terrorism and drug-trafficking; (g) Economic and commercial cooperation; (h) Promotion of friendly exchanges in various fields.[2] In the subsequent dialogues, invariably these issues became the main focus. In 1998, again the same eight issues were identified including Peace, Security and Confidence Building Measures; Jammu & Kashmir; Siachen; Wullar Barrage/Tulbul Navigation Project; Terrorism and Drug Trafficking; Economic and Commercial Cooperation; and Friendly Exchanges in Various Fields.[3] The MoU signed between the Foreign Secretaries at the end of the Lahore Summit expanded these items to include a number military and nuclear CBMs. To a large extent, there is an agreement between both countries on issues that need to be focused, starting with Jammu & Kashmir.

India and Pakistan should try to discover what is the most painful cause of their conflict; Siachen Glacier, Wullar Barrage/Tulbul Navigation Project, cross-border militancy or Kashmir. In other words, they should structure their bilateral conflicts and prioritize them according to the importance, human, economic and political costs, calculated benefits (in future) of their conflict. This structure should be made with mutual consensus.

III. TO NEGOTIATE A TABLE AND A TIME-TABLE

Second, India and Pakistan should identify the modalities of approaching the conflict including Kashmir. After agreeing to negotiate, both countries in the past have faced problems in agreeing on the modalities.[4] In the last two decades, there have been thirteen rounds of bilateral talks at the Foreign Secretary level.

[2] See Joint Statement, *The Hindu*, 24 June 1997. Also see <http://meaindia.nic.in/jk/jps.htm>

[3] 'India, Pak Agree on Calendar for Talks', *The Hindu*, 18 September 1998.

[4] 'Let's Forget Modalities and Resume Talks: Aziz', *The Hindustan Times*, 3 September 1998; 'India, Pak Agreement on Talks', *The Hindustan Times*, 4 September 1998.

Between 1984 and 1998 alone, there were twelve rounds of bilateral talks at their level.[5] India and Pakistan invariably have fallen on bilateral talks on the Foreign Secretary level resulting in establishing Joint Working Groups (JWG) on various issues, only to reach a deadlock.

It was decided in September 1998 that 'all outstanding issues shall be dealt with at the levels indicated below: Peace and security including CBMs (Foreign Secretaries), Jammu & Kashmir (Foreign Secretaries), Siachen (Defence Secretaries), Wullar Barrage/ Tulbul Navigation Project (Secretaries, Water and Power), Sir Creek (Additional Secretary (Defence)/Surveyor General), Terrorism and Drug Trafficking (Home/Interior Secretaries), Economic and Commercial Cooperation (Commerce Secretaries), promotion of friendly exchanges in various fields (Secretaries, Culture).'[6] After the Lahore Summit in 1999, it was decided that the foreign secretaries of Pakistan and India would meet at the end of March or in early April 1999 for a new 'round of their talks on Kashmir and peace and security while the Foreign Ministers will meet within a month of that meeting', and later the foreign ministers would 'review the progress of the dialogue on the bilateral agenda in any case . . . and there may be other dimensions which might come up'.[7]

By the first week of March, however, there were clear signs of the dialogue process wilting under pressure. Nawaz Sharif wanted to resolve the Kashmir conflict within a specific timeframe, while Vajpayee reiterated that India would not lose any more territory.[8] There were reports of Pakistan threatening to use 'other means' if its demand was not met.[9] Though there were positive developments, the process could not proceed further. Both countries

[5] J.N. Dixit, 'Untying the Gordian Knot', *The Hindustan Times*, 19 August 1998.

[6] 'Text of Joint Statement Made by Indo-Pak Foreign Secys', *The Hindu*, 25 September 1998.

[7] 'Foreign Secys Meet by March-end: Aziz', *The Hindu*, 25 February 1999.

[8] See 'Tough Talks Replaces Bonhomie', *The Pioneer*, 1 March 1999; 'We will not Loose any more Territory, Says PM', *The Hindu*, 1 March 1999; 'War of Words Stalls Indo-Pak Dialogue', *The Asian Age*, 2 March 1999.

[9] 'Pak to Resort to Other Means if Talks Fail', *The Hindu*, 1 March 1999.

agreed to free civilian prisoners;[10] India announced its willingness to reopen the Kokhrapar border;[11] the bus between Lahore and New Delhi became functional;[12] the Pakistan Foreign Office gave permission to the Indian High Commission to issue thousand visas for Pakistani fans to watch the Indo-Pak cricket match at Mohali;[13] and there were even reports of troops pulling out from Siachen.[14] The Foreign Minister of Pakistan, Mr Sartaj Aziz, and the Minister of External Affairs of India, Jaswant Singh met at Nuwara Eliya, Sri Lanka and agreed to start the next round of the dialogue process in May 1999 in New Delhi and Islamabad for a period of six weeks.[15] The eruption of Kargil conflict subsequently ended the Lahore initiative.

The 1998 process raised much expectations, only to let the people of both countries down. The Foreign Secretaries met in Islamabad and later in New Delhi during November 1998. Invariably, on all the issues, both sides stuck to their stated positions. Though both countries agreed to continue their discussion on the Tulbul project, it was evident that the talks on the issue were deadlocked.[16] Though there was a lot of expectation on Siachen,[17] there was more hostility than any understanding be-

[10] 'India, Pak to Free Civilian Prisoners', *The Hindu*, 7 March 1999; subsequently, civilians were freed later in March 1999. See 'India, Pak Exchange Prisoners', *The Hindu*, 23 March 1999.

[11] 'India is Ready to Open Sindh Border', *The Asian Age*, 10 March 1999.

[12] 'First Batch of Passengers Arrives from Lahore', *The Hindu*, 17 March 1999.

[13] 'Pak Grants Permission for Cricket Fans', *The Hindu*, 27 March 1999.

[14] 'Talks Likely on Troop Pullout', *The Hindustan Times*, 18 March 1999.

[15] 'Indo-Pak Dialogue Must Go On', *The Hindu*, 20 March 1999.

[16] See 'India, Pak to Continue Talks on Tulbul Project', *The Hindu*, 6 November 1998; 'India and Pakistan Agree to Disagree Even on Water', *Economic Times*, 6 November 1998; 'Pakistan, India Fail to Resolve Tulbul Dispute', *The Times of India*, 6 November 1998; 'Indo-Pak Tulbul Talks a Washout', *The Pioneer*, 6 November 1998.

[17] See Bharat Bhushan, 'High Altitude War that is Most Wasteful and Futile', *The Hindustan Times*, 6 November 1998; 'Siachen Issue will be Discussed Afresh', *The Asian Age*, 6 November 1998; Gaurav C. Sawant, 'War with no Winners', *The Indian Express*, 7 November 1998.

tween the two sides.[18] Dialogue on Sir Creek too failed to reach any consensus, and both the countries were divided whether it should be decided bilaterally or through external mediation.[19] The least complicated issue of all—trade, wilted under the pressure of the other failures.[20] When, L.K. Advani condemned the ISI for creating 'anarchy and instability' in India, the dialogue process, for all purposes was dead.[21]

Is the formation of JWGs led by Foreign Secretaries or Secretaries from other departments/ministries the ideal method of proceeding with the dialogue? Do these JWGs provide an ideal atmosphere in which the issues can be approached delicately? Is it possible to look beyond JWGs while discussing the critical issues? The structure and the mode of seeking a way out (seizure of a ripe moment through negotiations) is critical.

Given the inflexibility of the bureaucracies on both sides, India and Pakistan could consider expanding the negotiating teams to include outsiders, especially from the strategic community and civil society. Instead of Joint Working Groups, there could be Joint Consultation Groups (JCG), consisting official representatives from the respective bureaucracies along with members from the strategic community and prominent non-political individuals who are respected on both sides.

Third, besides identifying the issues and modalities of negotiation, it is essential to have a fixed timetable for various JCGs,

[18] See 'Hostility Flares up During Indo-Pak Talks on Siachen', *The Times of India*, 7 November 1998; 'Pakistan Rejects India's Siachen Ceasefire Plan', *The Hindu*, 7 November 1998; 'Siachen Talks Go the Tulbul Way', *The Hindustan Times*, 7 November 1998; 'Siachen War of Words Stings India', *The Telegraph*, 7 November 1998.

[19] See 'No Headway in Indo-Pak Talks on Sir Creek Dispute', *The Times of India*, 10 November 1998; 'Indo-Pak Talk and Deadlock Continues', *The Economic Times*, 10 November 1998; 'Sir Creek: Talks Fail, Pak for Arbitration', *The Indian Express*, 10 November 1998; 'India Rejects Pak Move on Sir Creek Issue', *The Hindu*, 10 November 1998.

[20] Pakistan Links Trade to Peace, Security', *The Times of India*, 11 November 1998; 'Trade Ties Linked to Political Breakthrough', *The Telegraph*, 11 November 1998; 'Peace First, then MFN Status', *The Asian Age*, 11 November 1998.

[21] 'Advani Back to Pak-bashing, says ISI Spread All Over India', *The Indian Express*, 12 November 1998.

independent of the other. One reason for the failure of previous dialogues has been that they were structured so closely in terms of time, that negative movement in one, affected the other. It is essential to de-link one process from the other in terms of time, so that they are insulated from any negative fallout from the other. In fact, a detached timeframe for different processes would give adequate time for both governments to plan better.

IV. .CORE OR OTHERWISE DON'T IGNORE KASHMIR

In particular, a JCG needs to be established on Jammu & Kashmir, having its own timetable. There is no doubt that Kashmir continues to be the core issue between India and Pakistan. While it is impossible to suggest any readymade solutions, the best approach would be to encourage both countries to engage in a process that would eventually lead to a peaceful resolution of the problem. The JCG could include representatives from the government and also from the civil society representing India, Pakistan and both sides of Kashmir. These negotiations could take place at Track 1½ level based on R.K. Mishra–Niaz Naik model.[22] The process needs to take place at four levels; between New Delhi and Islamabad, New Delhi and Srinagar, Islamabad and Muzaffarabad, and Srinagar and Muzaffarabad.

While the emphasis should be on the process and not on the solution, there would be nothing wrong to focus on possible compromises. There have been a number of solutions which have been floated by various organizations and individuals.

It is worth considering the deliberations of a small group of Indians and Pakistanis on Kashmir, who met at Shanghai.[23] The

[22] Suba Chandran and Rizwan Zeb, 'Taking the Indo-Pak Peace Process Further', *IPCS Policy Brief 2*, March 2004.

[23] The Regional Centre for Strategic Studies (RCSS), Colombo organized a workshop at Shanghai in December 2003. A joint group was constituted to look into the Kashmir issue and suggest possible outcomes. The RCSS Kashmir Group (RKG) submitted a proposal during the final day of the workshop, which can be accessed at the RCSS website. See 'Kashmir: What Next', in *Defence, Technology and Cooperation in South Asia*, Report on the Proceeding of Tenth Workshop, pp. 56–61. The report can be accessed at http://www.rcss.org/summerboook.pdf

RCSS Kashmir Group (RKG) concluded 'that two autonomous Kashmirs with a soft border would be a compromise that could be sold to every side that is involved in the conflict'.[24] According to the report produced by the group:[25]

> Both the Kashmirs would be given maximum autonomy from Indian and Pakistani side. The control of India and Pakistan would be limited to defence, currency and communication. There would be two autonomous Kashmir regions with two different autonomous governments, looking after the affairs of the region.
>
> The Line of Control would be made into a soft border. People and goods from both sides of Kashmir would be allowed to cross freely. Communication links would be enhanced and trade would be allowed freely. They would travel across under Kashmiri documents through the checkpoints. However, Indian and Pakistani nationals, other than Kashmiris would need adequate visa requirements to cross into other parts of Kashmir. For example an Indian national would need no document to visit the Indian side of Kashmir, but would need proper document to visit Pakistan's side of Kashmir.

Thus the following needs to be considered; time framework, type/mode of negotiations and political language to be used during a dialogue. At what level, on what basis, with whom, should negotiations be conducted. Both parties should work on a timeframe of dialogue. The mechanism of negotiations should be outlined in a way that would be acceptable to the parties. Whether it is a year long plan or more, the time period for negotiations should strictly be specified along with its target orientations (agreements, accords, etc.). Supporting structural settings of negotiations, an analyst suggests 'a set of CBMs; their gradual and faithful implementation according to a time schedule; ongoing parleys and negotiations; the public desire to support their government's peace efforts; ceasing hostile propaganda and armed hostilities (across borders); not abetting internal disorder (within each other's territories) through proxy wars; and promoting non-political (educational, cultural, social and travel) links. Most importantly it has to be a result-oriented exercise

[24] See 'Kashmir: What Next', p. 59.

[25] Ibid.

within a fixed timeframe in order to be termed a "success".'[26]

It seems important to decide the mode or type of talks, bilateral or multilateral. It depends upon the suitability and comfort of the parties whether they can pursue their objectives under a trilateral framework or bilateral. If they opt for multilateral talks or particularly mediation, they should look for an impartial facilitator without having any strategic or political stakes in the region. Moreover, India and Pakistan should agree on the primary cause of their conflict. Throughout the history of their peace processes, it is evident that they have had serious quarrels over the political terms they used during negotiations. 'Kashmir' or 'cross-border terrorism' are two sides of the same coin. They should also avoid blaming each other.

If India needs to agree on a JCG on Kashmir, then Pakistan also needs to agree on what India consider as the core issue—cross-border terrorism. India has been accusing Pakistan, at the highest levels, of aiding cross-border terrorism in Kashmir to abetting terrorist acts elsewhere in the country. For example, India has blamed Pakistan for some of the most significant terrorist attacks in the recent past. Pakistan was blamed for the hijacking of the Indian Airlines airplane from Kathmandu to Kandhar in December 1999.[27] Even Vajpayee accused Pakistan for the same, while Pakistan rejected it as baseless.[28]

V. IMPROVING TRADE

Fourth, both India and Pakistan should identify the areas of their economic cooperation. Mutual collaboration in the areas of trade, business, water resources, energy, environment, transport and com-

[26] Dr Maqsoodul Hassan Noori, 'Quest for Conflict Resolution in South Asia and Mid-East: Promise and Pitfalls', *Spotlight* (Islamabad), vol. XVIII, no. 5, May 1999. Cited in Shaheen Akhtar, op. cit., p. 49.

[27] See 'We have Evidence against Pak, says Brajesh', *The Hindu*, 3 January 2000; 'Hijackers Identified; Pak Hand Confirmed', *The Times of India*, 7 January 2000; 'Pak had "Prior Knowledge" of IA Plane Hijack', *The Hindu*, 10 January 2000; 'Hijack Plot was Hatched in Pak', *The Hindustan Times*, 23 January 2000.

[28] 'Hijackers are Not Our Nationals, says Pakistan', *The Times of India*, 3 January 2000; 'India Wants Pak to be Declared a Terrorist State', *The Times of India*, 4 January 2000.

munications, poverty alleviation, employment generation, etc., can help them in bridging their gaps. In case of India and Pakistan, the official trade amounts to a meagre $ 120 million—since 1994—in comparison to their combined global trade of $ 72 billion, and has shown practically no substantial increase over the years.[29] Though there is about $1 billion informal trade between the two countries, the growth in intra-regional trade would make a dramatic difference if cross-border trade in the region were legalized.[30] Both India and Pakistan could also play a role in encouraging intra-regional economic cooperation throughout South Asia. It may lead to realization of potential economic benefits from: lower intra-regional transport and transaction costs; more favourable terms of trade; economies of scale in investment, production and distribution, and possibly higher efficiencies due to increased external and intra-regional trade creation.[31]

The business community in India and Pakistan has been requesting for a long time for 'freeing the trade'.[32] According to Jagdish Khattar, who led a Confederation of Indian Industry (CII) delegation in 2001 to Pakistan, 'legal bilateral trade is somewhere in the region of $ 220–250 million, while illegal trade, primarily through Dubai and Singapore is at least 4–6 times higher', and if Pakistan could grant MFN status to India, the bilateral trade could go up to $ 5 billion in a short span of time.[33] Arun Jaitley, the India's Commerce Minister commented, 'The fact is that invisible trade between the two countries is already on. The need of the hour is to legitimize it to achieve its full potential.'[34] Most of the economists and businessmen are in fact concerned with the level of illegal trade between the two countries.[35]

[29] Noori, 'Quest for Conflict Resolution in South Asia and Mid-East: Promise and Pitfalls', p. 49.

[30] Shaheen Akhtar, p. 58.

[31] Debapriya Bhattacharya, 'Economic Confidence Building Measures in South Asia', in Dipanker Banerji (ed.), *CBMs in South Asia: Potential and Possibilities*, Sri Lanka: Regional Centre for Strategic Studies, 2000, p. 111.

[32] 'Call for freeing Indo-Pak trade', *The Business Line*, 7 September 2001.

[33] Ibid.

[34] 'Call for Improving Indo-Pak Trade', *Deccan Herald*, 3 March 2004.

[35] See Editorial, 'Fillip to Indo-Pak Trade Overdue', *The Statesman*, 14 August 2001.

Many in India believe that Pakistan's refusal to trade is more to do with political factors than economic. According to Mahendra P. Lama:

> The real reasons are the politically driven trade policy of Pakistan. Though tea is the top most item in the 601 freely importable list of Pakistan from India it is not imported from India. This is because the two major multinational tea trading companies in Pakistan have their tea gardens in Kenya and it is natural for them to make Pakistan a captive market. In this context the Kashmir issue is only a veil to justify the command over the market by the multinationals. As a result of all these restrictions, a large-scale unauthorized trade takes place along the 625-mile long border with India'.[36]

Despite the need for improving the trade relations, both countries have failed to move ahead due to their differences in approaching trade and security issues. India prefers to have trade first, presuming that it would improve the relations between the two countries, while, Pakistan prefers to resolve Kashmir conflict first, presuming that it would automatically lead to improved trade relations. This was explicit in the statements made by Indian External Affairs Minister, Yashwant Sinha and Aziz Ahmad Khan, Pakistan High Commissioner-designate, at an India-Pakistan trade meeting in New Delhi in July 2003.

Addressing business leaders from Pakistan at the third meeting of the India-Pakistan Chambers of Commerce and Industry (IPCCI), Sinha stated that economics should play a vital role in Indo-Pak bilateral relations, while Aziz Khan emphasized 'trade and economic cooperation flourish in an atmosphere of peace, amity and cooperation . . . low intra-regional trade in South Asia can only be attributed to the persistence of suspicion-prone and conflict-relations between the two major countries of the region—India and Pakistan'.[37]

Besides improving trade at a bilateral level, there has also been a realization that it will also result in enhancing the 'exchange of

[36] Mahendra P. Lama, 'Boosting Indo-Pak Trade', *The Hindustan Times*, 1 January 1999.

[37] 'Economics Must Play Dominant Role in Indo-Pak Ties: Sinha', *The Hindu*, 8 July 2003.

expertise and legislation on issues pertaining to the World Trade Organisation and anti-dumping'.[38]

Both India and Pakistan can explore economic grounds of cooperation by activating SAARC. The regional organization has, so far, failed to promote cooperation on regional basis due to political polemics between India and Pakistan. India and Pakistan should concentrate on areas of energy and gas resources. In area of energy cooperation, Pakistan could provide its overland routes to India for its imports and exports to Iran and Central Asian states. Pakistan can also help India to establish gas pipelines from Iran, Central Asia and Middle East via Pakistan. Likewise, India could allow transit facilities for Pakistan to trade with Bangladesh, Bhutan, Nepal and Sri Lanka.[39]

Fifth, a series of police and military CBMs need to take place, irrespective of movement on other areas of conflict. This dialogue and contacts should be on a permanent basis, irrespective of political fluctuations on both sides. Parallel meetings between the heads of intelligence services (ISI and RAW) should take place to ensure peace in areas of their jurisdiction.[40]

VI. LET THE PEOPLE MEET

There has been repeated emphasis on improving people-to-people contacts and emerging exchange of academics, scholars, policy-makers, economists and others. Steinberg, while analysing the Oslo Peace Process with reference to the ripeness model, discovers a fundamental missing element in that is, the 'bottom up transformation approach'. He views 'people-to-people contact' as a leading factor for motivational ripeness (precondition to ripeness). It produces greater trust at a societal level, which builds confidence

[38] Editorial, 'Fillip to Indo-Pak Trade Overdue', *The Statesman*, 14 August 2001.

[39] Siddiq, 'The Relevance of Economics and Environment in the South Asian Security', p. 95.

[40] 'The Beginning of the Future', Regional Perspective, Institute of Regional Studies (IRS), September 2000, a Joint Approach Paper by IRS, Islamabad and International Centre for Peace Initiatives, Mumbai/New Delhi, cited in Shaheen Akhtar, p. 55.

among people of the two sides. This enables the masses to give their consent for any government initiative towards peace. He also establishes links with mediation. He quotes Rothman: 'The role of the mediators and facilitators in such people-to-people exercises was based on models developed from individual and group psychology, with much lower emphasis on the political aspects of conflict transformation or the means to develop mutual understanding of conflicting group interests'.[41] India and Pakistan can also adopt this approach and that will reduce the enemy image of the two countries. Though since October 2003, people-to-people contacts have increased, as shall be seen subsequently, and especially during and after the Indo-Pak cricket matches, there were severe visa regimes and in most cases, the visas were city specific.

People-to-people contacts should be institutionalized at all levels. In particular, an exchange of parliamentarians, academicians, journalists and students from both sides will play a vital role in improving relations between the two countries.[42] While an exchange of people at all levels should be welcomed, emphasis should be especially added to these specific groups, as they would make a huge impact in the long run. A leading commentator in India observing the importance of the dialogue between the societies stated that, 'without a broader engagement between the two civil societies on war and truce as well as development and good governance, there will be no lasting peace and co-operation between the two nations.'[43] There were a number of instances in which India and Pakistan have rejected visas even for writers and poets. In January 2003 India denied visas to thirteen Punjabi writers from Pakistan who wanted to attend the International Punjabi Writers Conference in New Delhi.[44]

[41] 'Steinberg Unripeness and Conflict Management: Re-examing the Oslo Process and its Lessons', p. 3.

[42] See Suba Chandran and Rizwan Zeb, 'Taking the Indo-Pak Peace Process Further'.

[43] C. Raja Mohan, 'Inviting Benazir Bhutto?', *The Hindu*, 1 February 2001.

[44] 'Pak Writers Denied Visa', *The Hindu*, 12 January 2003.

Should the visa regimes be liberalized only after bilateral consultation or should it be undertaken unilaterally by one country irrespective of the other? I.K. Gujral, former Prime Minister of India observed:

> Security compulsions do require some caution, all the same, we must know that terrorists and outlaws do not come through established legal channels that require visas. While a more relaxed visa policy serves our national interests, I also feel that there is an urgent need for an attitudinal change at the immigration booths at the airports, and at Wagah, where every incoming guest must be treated with dignity and honour. And we must unilaterally end or drastically revise the rules regarding reporting to the police stations.[45]

The visa restrictions have been a major irritant in civil society in both countries interacting easily and freely. Admiral (Retd) Ramdas of the Indian Navy, also the President of the Indian chapter of Pakistan-India People's Forum for Peace and Democracy (PIPFPD) stated 'that restricting citizens mobility' 'would only stifle the civil society's attempts at reuniting the people of India and Pakistan through people-to-people dialogue and peace initiatives.'[46]

Whenever the visa regime has been relaxed, the traffic between the two countries has been heavy, leading to good will and a better atmosphere. During April–May 2000, there were two groups from India and Pakistan visiting each other. The Pakistani team that came to India, led by Asma Jehangir stated that they hated two nations addressing each other as enemy countries.[47] Another team visited Jawaharlal Nehru University, New Delhi in the same year, in which a school student, when asked to share his experience in India stated 'I came here to see how my enemies look. I'm still to find one'.[48] One direct implication of any such visits

[45] 'Should we Liberalise Visas for Pakistanis?' *The Times of India*, 30 December 2000.

[46] 'Pak-India Forum Disapproves of Visa Restrictions', *The Hindu*, 3 January 2003.

[47] 'Throw open Wagah, there will be Traffic Jams', *The Hindu*, 3 May 2000.

[48] The meeting was hosted by the South Asia Studies Division, JNU in 2001, in which one of the researcher was present.

between the two societies is the emphasis on peace. A group of Pakistani poets, artists, academics and journalists after meeting their counterparts in India even went ahead and suggested that both countries should pursue peaceful negotiations to resolve all conflicts including Kashmir and that both countries should abolish weapons of mass destruction.[49]

What became apparent during the recent Indo-Pak cricket matches was the existence of warmth towards each other at the grassroot level. More than the cricket matches, it is the interaction between people that generated enormous good feeling. According to an Indian cricket fan, who went to watch the one day matches in Karachi and Rawalpindi, all his initial apprehensions and opinions about Pakistan and Pakistanis were shattered when he interacted with the common folk both inside and outside the stadiums.[50] Another commented that the local population took additional efforts to make them (Indians) feel comfortable. He narrated an incident in which when he was standing in a long queue, wearing Indian T-shirt, to collect mineral water bottles in Lahore, he was requested to jump the queue.[51] A college student from University of Delhi, who went to Pakistan for the first time, was surprised to find the others very much like him and commented 'all these days, these guys (political leadership in India) have been fooling us. The people (of Pakistan) and not the cricket matches are a revelation'.[52] A former government employee, who has visited Pakistan previously felt, that there has been a genuine change in the society in the last few years and stated that the goodwill and warmth can no way be orchestrated.[53]

Personal interactions with people who have visited Pakistan during the cricket matches, correspond to the reports that have been published in newspapers and magazines during March–April 2004. Tanvir Ahmad Khan, the former Foreign Secretary of Pakistan has been quoted saying that, 'the main significance of

[49] 'Pakistan Scholars Pledge Peace, Not War', *The Asian Age*, 28 November 2000.

[50] Personal interview with an Indian cricket fan.

[51] Personal interviews.

[52] Ibid.

[53] Ibid.

what is happening in cricket stadiums is the release of pent up emotions. It's positive emotion on display in both countries. They are saying, we want to move forward and fast.'[54]

People have been always willing to visit and host each other. Even, many of those who came to India as refugees during Partition have many fond memories of their birthplace.[55] Majority of the refugee families (who are well settled now in India) who were interviewed answered that they would be too happy to visit Pakistan if given a chance.[56] Though they are not interested in shifting back, they showed interest in visiting the places and meeting their erstwhile neighbours.[57] A shopkeeper in South Delhi, who came to India during Partition and witnessed violence to his own family stated that he would not mind sending his son to have a branch in Pakistan.[59] A retired military personnel commented that had Partition been planned in a better manner, his family would have even stayed back in Pakistan.[59]

There are many young scholars in India who would like to visit Pakistan to understand it better and also to conduct research. Unfortunately, adequate scholarships for scholars to undertake research in Pakistan are not available. Many scholars who were interviewed, irrespective of their discipline showed an interest in visiting Pakistan.[60] Such visits would generate enormous goodwill, besides their personal interaction with the other, improving their understanding about each other. It is unfortunate that many of the researchers who are working exclusively on Pakistan in

[54] Mariana Baabar, 'Pakistan Smiling', *Outlook*, 29 March 2004, p 69.

[55] The fondness towards the other was observed more among the elder generation who witnessed Partition. Strangely, the present generation does not share the same fondness, though there is no explicit hostility towards Pakistan that was expressed during the interviews. Personal interviews during January–March 2004.

[56] Personal interviews with families who came to India during Partition.

[57] Personal interviews during January–March 2004.

[58] Personal interview in February 2004.

[59] Personal interview in March 2004.

[60] One of the researchers conducted a series of interviews with the student community in Jawaharlal Nehru University and University of Delhi, two premier educational institutes in New Delhi. Invariably, every one wanted to visit Pakistan, irrespective of their academic backgrounds. Even students studying in the School of Languages in JNU showed enormous interest in visiting Pakistan.

premier research centres submitted their Ph.D. without even visiting the country once.[61]

It is essential that the academic community researching on India and Pakistan be encouraged to conduct field studies and exchange academic visits. There were incidents, in which the Governments of India and Pakistan took contrary steps. According to a news report, the Pakistan Government in November 2001, banned 'any assistance or cooperation between Pakistani and Indian educational and research institutions'.[62]

India and Pakistan could establish a foundation, on the model of the B.P. Koirala Foundation between India and Nepal, to facilitate people-to-people contact. Both countries could establish a Jinnah-Gandhi Foundation that would facilitate the exchanges of academics, students and others who have no political aspirations. It is unfortunate there are no formal academic exchanges of students between the two premier universities of India and Pakistan—Jawaharlal Nehru University, New Delhi and Quaid-i-Azam University, Islamabad. The Jinnah-Gandhi Foundation could provide scholarships to students who would like to study in other institutes, or to select journalists to visit each other for a specific period.[63] Universities apart, independent foundations could provide scholarships for the exchange of scholars from different fields for a shorter period to research in other countries. International foundations and non-governmental organizations could play a positive role in formalizing these exchanges, which could be supplemented by governmental exchanges mentioned earlier.[64]

Besides the academic community, the Parliamentarians of both countries should be provided ample opportunities to visit each

[61] In India, there are three premier centres, where exclusive studies on Pakistan is undertaken—South Asia Studies Division, JNU, Centre for South Asia Studies, University of Jaipur and Centre for South and South-East Asia Studies, University of Madras. There has always been enormous enthusiasm amongst the students in these centres in pursuing their M.Phil. and Ph.D. on Pakistan.

[62] The report originally appeared in the *Dawn*, and was reproduced in India. See 'Pak bans ties with Indian universities', *The Asian Age*, 7 November 2001.

[63] Suba Chandran and Rizwan Zeb, 'Taking the Indo-Pak Peace Process Further'.

[64] Ibid.

other. In the past, exchange of MPs from both sides have brought about a better atmosphere. The visit of a thirteen member delegation from Pakistan in May 2003 and the subsequent visit of an Indian team to Pakistan did not achieve anything spectacular but, provided the much needed exposure about the other. Kuldip Nayar, the leader of the Indian delegation, however was upset with the Pakistan Government's response, and stated, 'There is no doubt, the response is overwhelming. We have been treated with utmost respect, love and affection. People have gone out of the way to extend the hand of friendship.'[65]

New Delhi and Islamabad should also take steps to improve contacts at sports and games level to facilitate the movement of people to participate and support such events. International business groups could arrange Indo-Pak joint teams to play against the rest of the world. For example, given the importance associated with cricket, a joint Indo-Pak team against World XI would strengthen not only people-to-people level contacts, but also create a positive atmosphere in both the countries.[66] Cricket, of all the games and sports, became the main victim of Indo-Pak hostility, due to its popularity. The Indian Sports Minister was quoted stating: 'Sports and cross-border terrorism cannot go together. . . . How can we (India) send the cricket team to play in Pakistan, when they are supporting terrorist activities in Kashmir?'[67]

Recent events would prove the importance of improving people-to-people contacts at the grass-root level.

VII. BUILDING CONFIDENCE ON NUCLEAR ISSUES

Both India and Pakistan need to set up Nuclear Risk Reduction Centres (NRRC), irrespective of progress in other areas. The NRRC could focus on the following:[68]

[65] 'Visiting Indian MPs Baffled by Pak Govt's Indifference', *The Times of India*, 23 June 2003.

[66] Suba Chandran and Rizwan Zeb, 'Taking the Indo-Pak Peace Process Further'.

[67] 'No Cricket with Pak: India', *The Hindu*, 8 December 2002.

[68] Suba Chandran and Rizwan Zeb, 'Taking the Indo-Pak Peace Process Further'.

- Prevent unintended signals from escalating to nuclear tension.
- Provide channels for instant communication between technical experts in the event of an accidental or any untoward incident.
- Identify, negotiate and implement any other procedural arrangements intended to reduce the risk of recourse to nuclear weapons.
- Help build trust and confidence in the area of conflict resolution

The NRRCs are essential to provide nuclear stability at the bilateral level. They would remove doubts and suspicions over the nuclear intentions of each other, thus mainly averting the dangers of a nuclear war—accidental or deliberate. Establishment of NRRCs assume significance especially for the following factors. The primary concern among them is the safety and security of the nuclear arsenal, both in India and Pakistan. The security provisions of the nuclear installations in India and Pakistan cannot be considered absolutely safe and if the terrorists plan to attack them, it may not be difficult.[69] Any such attack would not only bring disaster but also initiate a nuclear war, given the mutual suspicion and mistrust. Besides the military nuclear installations, the civilian nuclear installations in India and Pakistan are also equally vulnerable to terrorist attacks.[70]

India and Pakistan, though party to the Convention on the Physical Protection of Nuclear Materials (PPNM) and IAEA, not all of their nuclear reactors are under IAEA safeguards. The IAEA safeguards primarily account for monitoring the use of nuclear material for peaceful purposes and do not protect then from theft or sabotage by 'unauthorized persons'.[71] With high level mis-

[69] While most of the alarming reports on the safety and security on nuclear installations in India and Pakistan have been published in the western media (perhaps even with an ulterior motive), the fact that these installations are vulnerable to militant attacks cannot be completely ruled out. A missile or car bomb or a suicide bomb attack of a nuclear installation in one country may raise the panic in the other.

[70] Arian L. Pregenzer, 'Securing Nuclear Capabilities in India and Pakistan', *Non Proliferation Review*, Spring 2003.

[71] George Bunn et al., 'Strengthening Nuclear Security', *Non Proliferation Review*, Fall/Winter 2001.

governance and corruption, as has been indicated by the recent Transparency International's *Global Corruption Report*, theft or unauthorized use cannot be ruled out in the case of India and Pakistan.

The NRRCs could play a positive role in building confidence over the command and control structure of nuclear weapons in India and Pakistan. These structures are robust and are in the process of evolution.[72] Besides, there have been serious doubts in the recent past over the issue of nuclear bureaucracy and its accountability to the state. There have been series of reports in the western media linking some of the Pakistani nuclear scientists with the al Qaeda and also with other countries.[73] The recent involvement of top nuclear scientists of Pakistan in the widespread proliferation of nuclear weapons and technology to North Korea, Libya and Teheran, raises doubts regarding the nuclear safety in the region.[74] Though no such incident has come to light in India, many in Pakistan do not rule out such a possibility. A series of reports at the national and international levels revealed the extent of involvement of Pakistan's nuclear bureaucracy in global nuclear

[72] For details see the following articles: Tanvir Ahmad Khan, 'Command and Control: A Pakistani Perspective', *Strategic Issues*, March 2000; Agha Shahi, 'Command and Control of Nuclear Weapons in South Asia', *Strategic Issues*, March 2000; P.R. Chari, 'Command and Control Arrangements' <http://www.ipcs.org/issues/articles/135-ndi-chari.html>; Zafar Iqbal Cheema, 'Pakistan's Nuclear Use Doctrine and Command and Control', in Peter Lavoy et al., *Planning the Unthinkable: How New Powers will use Nuclear, Biological and Chemical Weapons*, Ithaca: Cornell University Press, 2000.

[73] See David Albright and Holly Higgins, 'A Bomb for Ummah', *Bulletin of Atomic Scientists*, March–April 2003. Also see Kamran Khan and Molly Moore, '2 Nuclear Scientists Briefed bin Laden, Pakistanis Say', *Washington Post*, 12 December 2001; Peter Baker, 'Pakistani Scientist who Met bin Laden Failed Polygraphs', *Washington Post*, 3 March 2002.

[74] David E. Sanger and William J. Broad, 'Pakistani's Nuclear Earnings: $100 Million', *The New York Times*, 16 March 2004; Leonard Weiss, 'Pakistan: It's Deja Vu All Over Again', *Bulletin of the Atomic Scientists*, May–June 2004; 'Pakistan's Nuclear Dealings, Rogues Step In', *The Economist* 370, no. 8357, 10 January 2004, p. 22; Johanna Mcgeary, 'Inside the A-Bomb Bazaar', *Time* 163, no. 2, 19 January 2004, p. 18; Jim Hoagland, 'Pakistan's Nuclear Alibaba', *The Washington Post*, 10 February 2004; William J. Broad, David E. Sanger and Raymond Bonner, 'A Tale of Nuclear Proliferation: How Pakistani Built His Network', *The New York Times*, 12 February 2004.

proliferation.[75] The Government of Pakistan carried out an investigation into these allegations.[76] Many inside Pakistan called for a thorough probe and necessary action.[77] Though A.Q. Khan had confessed[78] and was removed from his special position as Special Advisor to the Prime Minister on Strategic Programme,[79] the issue is far from over. Though many in India considered the confession and apology a mere eyewash, the Government of India ignored the issue as an internal matter of Pakistan. The NRRCs could play a positive role during such crisis situations, reassuring the other.

Finally, the NRRCs also could play a positive role in terms of sharing the intelligence, so that the nuclear assets do not fall in the hands of militants. While it may be difficult for militant groups to produce Weapons of Mass Destructions (WMD), it may not be difficult to acquire them, given the laxity of command and

[75] See William J. Broad, David Rohde and David E. Sanger, 'Inquiry Suggests Pakistanis Sold Nuclear Secrets', *The New York Times*, 22 December 2003; Editorial, 'Pakistan's Nuclear Commerce', *The New York Times*, 23 December 2003; David E. Sanger and William J. Broad, 'From Rogue Nuclear Programs, Web of Trails Leads to Pakistan', *The New York Times*, 4 January 2004; Patrick E. Tyler and David E. Sanger, 'Pakistan Called Libyan's Source of Atom', *The New York Times*, 6 January 2004.

[76] See 'Pakistan Holds Scientists for Questioning', *The New York Times*, 13 December 2003; 'Pakistan Questions 8 Connected to Its Nuclear Program', *The New York Times*, 19 January 2004; 'More Nuclear Scientists Held for Questioning', *The News*, 19 January 2004; 'N-scientists Debriefing in National Interest: PM', *Dawn*, 23 January 2004; 'Government Decides to Punish Guilty Scientists', *The News*, 27 January 2004.

[77] Farrukh Saleem, 'Our Nuclear Quagmire', *The Friday Times*, 2–8 January 2004; Editorial, 'Pak Role in Proliferation', *The Nation*, 6 January 2004; Ayesha Siddqa, 'Dealing with Nuclear Bureaucracies in South Asia', *The Friday Times*, 9–15 January 2004; Editorial, 'Nuclear Issue', *The News*, 28 January 2004; Farhan Bokhari, 'Nuclear Questions', *The News*, 29 January 2004; Najam Sethi, 'Nuclear Shenanigans', *The Friday Times*, 30 January 2004–5 February 2004; Editorial, 'Coming Clean', *Dawn*, 31 January 2004; Mir Jamilur Rahman, 'Debriefing the Scientists,' *The News*, 31 January 2004; Imtiaz Alam, 'Nuclear Mess: A Powerful Probe Commission is Needed to Nab All the Holy Cows', *South Asia Tribune*, 1–7 February 2004; Editorial, 'The Law of the Land and A.Q. Khan', *Daily Times*, 2 February 2004.

[78] 'Dr Khan Seeks Pardon', *Dawn*, 5 February 2004.

[79] 'Dr Qadeer Removed from Adviser Post', *The News*, 1 February 2004.

control structures in South Asia. Currently, the main focus of terrorists, in terms of the use of weapons, has been that of machine guns and improvised explosive devices (IED). In the recent past, the terrorists in South Asia have refrained from carrying out any major attack that would kill innocent people at random, mainly due to the fear that such an action would alienate them from the local population. The targets are carefully chosen and in most cases, they have a political purpose. In most cases, the target has either been security forces, or persons belonging to the minority community or individuals close to the establishment.

Recent years have seen reports of thefts of radio active material from energy facilities. In May 2003, there were reports of Jamaat-ul-Mujahideen, a militant group in Bangladesh smuggling enough uranium to 'make a crude bomb.'[80] There have been at least four instances of seizure of nuclear fissile materials in India since June 1998.[81]

While al Qaeda's efforts to build or acquire WMD have been extensively researched,[82] what is yet to be focused is the linkages between al Qaeda and other militant organizations fighting in Pakistan and Kashmir. The existence of such a link would clearly indicate the possibility of the use of WMDs by terrorists in the region.

VIII. ENGAGING THE RIGHT

The rightist forces—both political parties and organizations in both countries have been opposed to any reconciliation with the other. Democratic and secular elements of civil society in both countries consider the rightist groups as an aberration and have

[80] M. Gargi, 'Uranium Heist', <http://www.ipcs.org/ipcs/issueIndex2.jsp?action=showView&kValue=1086&issue=1015&status=article&mod=b>

[81] Ibid.

[82] See the following: David Albright, 'al Qaeda's Nuclear Programme', http://www.nautilus.org/for a/Special-Policy-Forum/47_Albright html; David Albright, Kathryn Buelhler and Holly Higgins, 'bin Laden and the Bomb', *Bulletin of Atomic Scientists*, January–February 2002. Also see 'WMD Terrorism and Osama bin Laden' <http://cns.miis.edu/pubs/reports/bin-laden.htm>

been attempting sidelining them in the dialogue process. When the delegation from the Pakistan Parliament visited India in May 2003, after a meeting with them, Somnath Chatterjee, CPI-M leader stated that 'both sides agreed that fundamentalist forces existed in the two countries and were hampering the process of establishment of peace. These forces should be isolated'.[83]

It is essential to understand, that the rightist forces in both countries may not have political power to prevent both societies from meeting each other, but have adequate street power to scuttle them, by creating communal mayhem. In such a situation, the civil societies may find it difficult to engage each other, as the atmosphere gets emotionally charged. The more the rightist groups are isolated by civil society on both sides, the more they attempt to increase the divide between the latter. Any communal upheaval encroaches the secular and democratic space of the civil society which is attempting to reach out to the other. The strategy towards the rightist forces should then be engaging them and not isolating them.

Increasing isolation of the rightist groups from the bilateral dialogue has resulted in the past, in politicizing and communalizing even predominantly secular events. For example, an analysis of the rightist responses to Indo-Pak cricket matches, which is purely a secular subject, would reveal the enormity of the situation. The rightist forces in both countries reacted in a highly uncivilized manner to an event which is watched the most by the civil societies in both countries.

In a news report published in *The Hindu*, Masood Azhar, leader of the now banned Jaish-e-Muhammad announced in February 2001, that 'dead bodies will be returned if the Indian cricket team visits Pakistan'.[84] Jai Bhagwan Goel, the President of the Delhi unit of the Shiv Sena stated in March 2001, 'When Pakistan is actively supporting and training foreign mercenaries in its land

[83] 'Indian, Pakistani MPs for Isolation of Fundamentalists', *Hindustan Times*, 9 May 2003.

[84] 'Dead Bodies will be Returned if Cricket Team Visits Pak', *The Hindu*, 7 February 2001.

and then exporting them to Kashmir for spreading terrorism, how can we have any cricketing or any other sporting ties with it?'[85] Earlier in 1999, the Shiv Sena dug up the pitch at Ferozeshah Kotla Stadium, New Delhi, to oppose the Indo-Pak cricket match. The Shiv Sena's President Bal Thackeray described the event as an act of true patriotism, while Madhukar Sarpotdar Shiv Sena member of Parliament, stated that there was no crime committed.[86] Shiv Sena also claimed that it had constituted a 'task force' to disrupt the India-Pakistan cricket series, besides warning the Indian cricket players that they too would be targeted if they played against Pakistan.[87] In Mumbai, they ransacked the Board of Control for Cricket in India (BCCI) office and damaged the trophies.[88] Shiv Sena-affiliated cable television operators threatened to stop telecasting the India-Pakistan cricket series and boycott the ESPN sports channel.[89] Later in December 2003, Sena activists damaged the cricket pitch in Agra that was to host a veterans' match between India and Pakistan.[90]

The Indian government, under pressure from rightist forces, cancelled the Indian cricket team's proposed tour to participate in a cricket tournament in Sharjah. The Pakistan Cricket Board immediately threatened to severe all cricketing relations with India, while General Musharraf announced that he would take up the issue during his visit to attend the Agra Summit.[91] Irre-

[85] 'Sena not for Cricketing Ties with Pak', *The Hindu*, 24 March 2001.

[86] Praveen Swami, 'Spreading its Wings', *Frontline*, 16–29 January 1999.

[87] 'Sena Forms "Suicide Squad" ', *The Tribune*, 20 January 1999.

[88] 'Not Cricket! Sena Men Vandalise BCCI Office', *The Indian Express*, 20 January 1999.

[89] Praveen Swami, 'A Catalogue of Crime', *Frontline*, 30 January–12 February, 1999.

[90] According to the newsreport, 'the Yuva Shiv Sena also claimed that it had constituted a 51-member "suicide squad" to disrupt the match and they would conduct self immolation in front of the Prime Minister's house if the match was played.' See 'Sena Activists Damage Pitch in Agra', *The Hindu*, 19 December 2003.

[91] 'Pak Threatens to Cut Cricket Ties', *The Asian Age*, 28 March 2001; 'Musharraf to Discuss Cricket Relations', *The Hindu*, 1 June 2001.

spective of pressure from civil society, the government refused to send its team to the tournament.[92]

The Vishwa Hindu Parishad (VHP), another rightist organization have also been publicly opposed to any rapprochement with Pakistan. Ashok Singhal, the President of VHP, considered Vajpayee's talks offer in 2003 as a 'blunder' and threatened 'blunders can be committed and pardoned once or twice, not always'.[93]

How to engage the right-wing forces in dialogue? First, the leaders on both sides could address them to mellow down their rhetoric.

Second, the leaders should be allowed and encouraged to visit each other countries. The visit of Maulana Fazlur Rehman, chief of a faction of the Jamiat-e-Ulama-e-Islam to India had its own positive implications. Fazlur Rehman was perceived by Indians as enjoying 'considerable clout among most of the Pakistan based militant group in Kashmir.'[94] Fazlur Rahman stated repeatedly that he would support the peace process.[95] On converting the LoC into an international border, he was even reported to have mentioned in a television interview, 'If both the countries agree to it and it is also accepted by the people of Kashmir, we will not have any objection.'[96]

Third, one should also take into account the electoral compulsions of the rightist parties and underplay their sensitivities, instead of targeting with an objective to isolate them. The rightist

[92] Invariably every editorial in the Indian newspapers criticized Indian government's decision not to send its team to the Sharjah tournament in 2001. *The Hindu*, in its editorial commented that 'it would be a shame if the Indian cricket team is now prevented from taking part in a tournament by a Sports Minister who is (at best) totally confused or (at worst) completely unreasonable'. Editorial, 'Cricket and Politics', *The Hindu*, 2 June 2001.

[93] 'Talks Offer a "Blunder": Singhal', *The Hindu*, 26 April 2003.

[94] Aasha Khosa, 'Track II Diplomacy: Pak Ulema to Visit India', *The Indian Express*, 25 May 2001.

[95] See 'We Support the Path of Peace, says Fazlur Rehman', *The Hindu*, 19 July 2003; 'Peace, Dialogue Figure in PM's Talks with Fazlur', *The Hindu*, 21 July 2003.

[96] 'Fazlur Rehman Reiterates LoC can Become Border', *Hindustan Times*, 19 July 2003.

forces themselves underplay, once they realize the enormity of public support for good will. During the Indo-Pak cricket matches on March 2004, the rightist forces in India and Pakistan deliberately underplayed their hostility. There were no mass street protests or digging up the pitches. Tanvir Ahmad Khan was quoted stating 'the feeling in the rightwing camp (in Pakistan) is that it is more prudent for India and Pakistan to stand together and be better off while resisting outside pressure'.[97]

To begin with both states could engage the moderate rightwing groups and encourage its leaders to visit the other. While the VHP and Shiv Sena are against any rapprochement with Pakistan, the Rashtriya Swayamsevak Sangh (RSS) has supported the BJP efforts to engage Pakistan. Its leader Madan Das has commented that India 'could not think in isolation' and the RSS would 'welcome any policy of maintaining friendly ties with neighbouring countries'.[98] In fact, the spokesman of the RSS, stated in August 2003, if there was an occasion, K.S. Sudarshan, the chief of the RSS would visit Pakistan.[99]

To conclude, the time is ripe for both countries to resolve their bilateral conflict. However there are certain irritants, as seen above towards exploiting the ripe conditions. Both governments should address these irritants, so as to reach an understanding towards the final resolution of their conflict.

[97] Mariana Baabar, 'Pakistan Smiling', *Outlook*, 29 March 2004.
[98] 'RSS Backs Vajpayee's Peace Bid with Pakistan', *Hindustan Times*, 2 May 2003.
[99] 'RSS Chief to Visit Pakistan?', *The Hindu*, 15 August 2000.

CHAPTER 5

Towards Ripeness: Conclusions and Recommendations

Are the Indo-Pak conflicts ripe for resolution? Has the right moment arrived, so that both states and societies can pursue certain steps that would eventually lead to the resolution of the points of discord.

As seen in Chapter 2, both countries have reached a deadlock, which would resemble Zartman's mutually hurting stalemate (MHS) model. A closer look at Zartman's MHS model defines it as a continuing impasse, a ripe moment to seize, as it is a 'necessary precondition to seek an alternate option, i.e. negotiations.'

ISSUES, STATUS AND REASONS

Issue	Status	Reasons
Military Initiatives	Deadlocked	Neither side can impose a military solution on the other. Presence of nuclear weapons has added further problems.
Militancy Initiatives	Deadlocked	Militancy has failed to achieve anything substantial, except bleeding the Kashmiri society. Implications are now being felt in Pakistan too.
Counter-Militancy Initiatives	Deadlocked	Military operations against militancy have not completely arrested violence in Kashmir. Peace is still a far cry.
Political Initiatives	Deadlocked	Nothing much has been achieved the previous peace initiatives—Lahore, Agra and Islamabad.

Why, then have both parties not reached an understanding? Is the Zartman theory inapplicable to Indo-Pak conflicts? Is the condition not ripe to resolve then? As seen in the second and third chapters, Zartman's MHS is an incomplete model one in regard to the Indo-Pak situation, lacking supportive elements to bring a rational, realistic and practical solution or management to the conflict situation.

The supportive elements that Zartman does not address are: Preconditions to ripeness (realization of a deadlock by the parties), factors that can help parties to identify cause or 'core' of the conflict/deadlock or ongoing parleys, motivations to initiate a 'series' of 'target oriented' negotiations etc. The study also establishes a relevant link of the drawbacks of MHS model with Indo-Pak ripeness. Zartman terms 'ripeness as a necessary pre condition to negotiations'. It is one of the major shortcomings of MHS model that it does not deal with the preconditions to 'ripeness'. Ripeness as an element can lead negotiations but what leads to ripeness or identification of the deadlock, needs to lie made clear. There are certain preconditions to ripeness that may help the parties to realize the need to negotiate. Positive political motivations, i.e. regular meetings of the direct parties to the conflict (heads of the states, military personnel, policy-makers), diplomatic visits (Track I, II and III), established communication links (activate hotlines), positive role of official media, etc., are essential in the MHS model. With reference to Indo-Pak ripeness, both enjoyed ripe moments and tried to seize them but this did not bring about any permanent settlement of their differences because Indo-Pak ripeness did not contain any political or economic motivations. Economic and political preconditions motivate parties to build trust and confidence and to resolve their disputes.

The element of 'mutuality' under MHS model lacks clarity and objectivity. While confessing that both parties seize the ripe moment after feeling the pains of a hurting deadlock 'mutually', Zartman portrays an ideal situation. Realization of a hurting deadlock by both parties 'at the same time, with the same degree of seriousness' rarely happens in world politics. Even if seemingly, both parties express their willingness to seize the moment, it is difficult to judge the genuineness of their seriousness and sincerity. The reason lies in the different dynamics of the ripeness model, especially the entrapment model and mutually enticing opportunity model. For example, in October 2003, India and Pakistan proposed a series of measures for building trust and confidence, one can verify their genuineness and seriousness. Pakistan perceived Indian proposals through two dimensions; forthcoming state elections in India and upcoming SAARC Summit, 4–6 January 2004. India perceived Pakistani proposals as scoring points over Kashmiris. The two countries moved ahead with the proposals in the backdrop of SAARC Summit due in January 2004. The offer also raised suspicions because Kashmir has been a catchy slogan to win votes in elections for Indian leadership and get domestic support for Pakistani leadership. Under the scenario, one can be doubtful whether or not the parties are sincere and serious enough to break the ice and reconcile their differences through dialogue.

Another factor under MHS model is related to external and internal convictions. Zartman specifies external ripeness as a highly dependent element on internal conviction. But he does not explain the way through which internal ripeness could be achieved. He also does not suggest any alternative to materialize external ripeness in the absence of internal consent. The parties should look for internal ripeness to go ahead with external ripeness. In the absence of internal conviction, external ripeness may not produce long lasting solutions. There may not be any substitute to internal consent because government needs popular support from different segments of society. One of the important factors is identification of the core of the conflict. Ripeness model does not establish any criteria which the 'core' issue can be judged. Parties, in some cases, view the situations and conflicts through different perceptions. For instance, India perceives 'cross-border terrorism' as the core of its conflict with Pakistan, and Pakistan considers the status of Jammu & Kashmir as the basis of its differences with India. Both do not reach the bottomline of their conflict which presents the same story. These factors make ripeness a complex model due to which parties realize the ripe moment, and start negotiations, yet cannot bring about any permanent outcome.

The case study of the Indo-Pak conflict with reference to Zartman's MHS model concludes that India and Pakistan should seize their existing ripe moment along with supportive elements. MHS model needs to be pursued in the Indo-Pak conflict in a way that can help the two parties to overcome their domestic, regional and international challenges. The biggest challenge both countries have been facing is the conflict behaviour at the intra-party level. With a diverse population, both states are highly influenced by their respective domestic constituencies. Effective and positive role of the state in both countries can build trust at the grass-root level. It will help both states reduce their politico-military schizophrenia. It would also help them to promote internal ripeness/convictions.

RECOMMENDATIONS

Pursue a Rhetoric Restraint Regime[1]

Peace may be a far cry; solutions may not be anywhere in sight. Do not complicate the process by indulging in unnecessary rhetoric. Rhetoric at Indo-Pak level, does not contribute anything positively, but harms the process immensely. It undermines the peace efforts and the peace constituencies in both societies. Second, it strengthens the hawkish elements enabling them to reiterate 'We have been telling so.' Third, it vitiates the civil society, with the media, especially the vernacular, fanning it. Any statement is followed by a counter—statement not only at the state level, but also at the popular level, with the rightist and militant sections in both countries making points and counterpoints. Avoid unnecessary statements at the governmental level. Pursue a strict rhetoric restraint regime.

[1] The phrase 'rhetoric restrain regime' was used by Pakistan's Foreign Minister in 2003.

Form a Panel Incorporating Track II

All the previous dialogues have been on Track I level mainly culminating in JWGs led by the bureaucracies from both sides. Allow Track II to take part in Track I meetings. This would reduce official hostility and rigidity. Allowing Track II in these meetings has an additional advantage. Unlike Track I, Track II meetings have been taking place for a longer period and have developed a personal rapport and understanding. Allowing Track II would not only reduce rigidity and hostility, but also provide a better and cordial atmosphere for the meetings.

Create Compartmentalized and Insulated Dialogues

Convert the dialogue process into a series of processes with independent time-table and meetings. Let there be a series of dialogues, instead of a single overarching dialogue. These dialogues could be on various issues that both countries find significant. Let these dialogues be also insulated from each other, so that a negative consensus on one process does not affect the other.

Emphasize the Importance of Kashmir and Terrorism

Kashmir and terrorism are two significant or 'core' issues for Pakistan and India respectively. Avoid unnecessary focus on what constitutes the core and emphasize the importance and significance of both issues and form panels exclusively to discuss both these issues.

Include the Kashmiris

Include the Kashmiris, directly or indirectly. The bus between the capitals of the two Kashmirs is a good beginning. Expand this process of meetings between the two Kashmirs at various levels—social, economic and political.

Focus on the Process Rather than the Product

Initial emphasis needs to be on the process and not on conflict resolutions. How to create and strengthen the process needs to be the immediate concern and not what should be reached at the end of the process.

Engage the Right

The rightist forces in both countries be tackled only by engaging them in the dialogue process rather than isolating them. Allow the political right to visit the other country and allow them to meet political leaders and people across the border.

Allow Sincere Facilitation, if There is Any

The Indo-Pak conflict has been exploited by the great powers during the Cold War era. Both had two major accords to resolve their differences;Tashkent Declaration and Simla Agreement.These accords did not bring any final solution. Soviet mediation could not prevent the two side going to another war in 1971. Indo-Pak ripeness lacked the motivational role of 'honest brokers'. Had they been capable enough to build people-to-people confidence to resolve Indo-Pak differences, India won't have been involved in the East Pakistan crisis in 1971. If India and Pakistan feel confident that the external environment is changed and could make use of external facilitation, both countries should explore that option.

Emphasize Regional Economic Growth

At the regional level, India and Pakistan should follow contemporary trends of regionalism. Keeping in view the phenomenon of economic regionalism, both should move with economic proposals. The economic and political motivations can enable the two to explore their areas of mutual collaboration. It can also help them to reach an amicable ground for talks. It will also be helpful for their smaller neighbours.

APPENDIX I

Meetings between the Prime Minister of India and the Prime Minister/President of Pakistan since 1972

Date	Venue	India	Pakistan
2 July 1972	Simla	Indira Gandhi	Z.A. Bhutto
31 Aug. 1978	Nairobi	Morarji Desai	Zia-ul-Haq
18 Apr. 1980	Salisbury`	Indira Gandhi	Zia-ul-Haq
1 Nov. 1982	New Delhi	Indira Gandhi	Zia-ul-Haq
10 Mar. 1983	New Delhi	Indira Gandhi	Zia-ul-Haq
4 Nov. 1984	New Delhi	Rajiv Gandhi	Zia-ul-Haq
13 Mar. 1985	Moscow	Rajiv Gandhi	Zia-ul-Haq
23 Oct. 1985	NewYork	Rajiv Gandhi	Zia-ul-Haq
18 Nov. 1985	Oman	Rajiv Gandhi	Zia-ul-Haq
7 Dec. 1985	Dhaka	Rajiv Gandhi	Zia-ul-Haq
17 Dec. 1985	New Delhi	Rajiv Gandhi	Zia-ul-Haq
15 Mar. 1986	Stockholm	Rajiv Gandhi	Mohd. Khan Junejo
17 Nov. 1986	Bangalore	Rajiv Gandhi	Mohd. Khan Junejo
21 Feb. 1987	New Delhi	Rajiv Gandhi	Zia-ul-Haq
4 Nov. 1987	Kathmandu	Rajiv Gandhi	Mohd. Khan Junejo
20 Aug. 1988	Islamabad	R. Venkataraman (President)	Ghulam Ishaq Khan
29–31 Dec. 1988	Islamabad	Rajiv Gandhi	Benazir Bhutto
July 1989	Islamabad	Rajiv Gandhi	Benazir Bhutto
22 Nov. 1990	Male	Chandrasekhar	Nawaz Sharif
24 May 1991	New Delhi	Chandrasekhar	Nawaz Sharif
17 Oct. 1991	Harare	Narasimha Rao	Nawaz Sharif
21 Dec. 1991	Colombo	Narasimha Rao	Nawaz Sharif
2 Feb. 1992	Davos	Narasimha Rao	Nawaz Sharif
14 June 1992	Rio-de-Janeiro	Narasimha Rao	Nawaz Sharif
3 Sep. 1992	Jakarta	Narasimha Rao	Nawaz Sharif
11 Apr. 1992	Dhaka	Narasimha Rao	Nawaz Sharif
2 May 1995	New Delhi	Narasimha Rao	Farooq Ahmed Leghari

(contd.)

APPENDIX I (contd.)

Date	Venue	India	Pakistan
12 May 1997	Male	I.K. Gujral	Nawaz Sharif
23 Sep. 1997	New York	I.K. Gujral	Nawaz Sharif
25 Oct. 1997	Edinburgh	I.K. Gujral	Nawaz Sharif
15 Jan. 1998	Dhaka	I.K. Gujral	Nawaz Sharif
29 July 1998	Colombo	A.B. Vajpayee	Nawaz Sharif
29 July 1998	New York	A.B. Vajpayee	Nawaz Sharif
20–21 Feb. 1999	Lahore	A.B. Vajpayee	Nawaz Sharif
July 2001	Agra	A.B. Vajpayee	Pervez Musharraf

Source: <http://www.meadev.nic.in/agra-summit/chr-sum.htm>

APPENDIX II

Major Agreements between India and Pakistan since Simla Agreement[1]

Date and Venue	Leaders of India and Pakistan	Agreements/Understandings
New Delhi, 1 Nov. 1982	Indira Gandhi & Zia-ul-Haq	Decision to form a Joint Commission to discuss bilateral issues. Decision to continue discussions on the 'mutual guarantees of non-aggression and non-use of force'[2] proposals and 'Peace, Friendship and Cooperation'[3] proposals that were circulated earlier by Pakistan and India respectively.
New Delhi, 10 Mar. 1983	Indira Gandhi & Zia-ul-Haq	Establishment of a Joint Commission to discuss various issues between India and Pakistan.[4]
Islamabad, 29-31 Dec. 1988	Rajiv Gandhi and Benazir Bhutto	Signing of three bilateral agreements: Prohibition of attack on each other's nuclear installations and facilities. Cultural Cooperation. Avoidance of double taxation on incomes derived.

(contd.)

[1] Suba Chandran, 'Limited War with Pakistan: Will it Secure India's Interests?'. ACDIS Occassional Paper, August 2004.

[2] Pakistan formally proposed a set of suggestions in April 1981 to India, when the conflict in Afghanistan was peaking on non-aggression and non-use of force. In June 1982, Pakistan revised the same proposal, after incorporating some suggestions from India.

[3] After receiving the June 1982 non-aggression proposals of Pakistan, India formally proposes a 'Treaty of Peace, Friendship and Cooperation' in August 1982, instead of a non-aggression pact.

[4] The first meeting of the Joint Commission took place on 4 June 1983, in which it was decided to form sub-commissions on economic relations, information, education, travel and tourism.

APPENDIX II (contd.)

Date and Venue	Leaders of India and Pakistan	Agreements/Understandings
Islamabad, 16–17 July 1989	Rajiv Gandhi and Benazir Bhutto	Joint Communiqué expressing the desire to work towards a comprehensive settlement to reduce he chances of conflict and avoidance of the use of force.
Male, 21–23 Nov. 1990	Chandrashekhar and Nawaz Sharif	Decision to set-up an additional hot-line between the two leaders. Decision to resume talks at Foreign Secretary levels.[5]
Male, 12 May 1997	I.K. Gujral and Nawaz Sharif	Decision to reactivate the hotline. Decision to constitute Joint Working Groups on various issues between India and Pakistan.[6]
Lahore, 20–21 Feb. 1999	A.B. Vajpayee and Nawaz Sharif	Lahore Declaration and Memorandum of Understanding (MoU) between the Foreign Secretaries of India and Pakistan.

[5] As a result of this meeting, the Foreign Secretaries met in December 1990 and agreed to evolve a 'bilateral code of conduct on treatment of diplomats'.

[6] Joint Working Groups (JWG) were formed to discuss Kashmir, Peace and Security, Siachen, Wular Barrage, Sir Creek, Terrorism and Drug Trafficking, Economic Cooperation, and Promotion of Friendly Ties. The talks at JWGs level broke down in September 1997, when Pakistan insisted on Kashmir as the core issue.

APPENDIX III

Jammu & Kashmir Time Line since the 2002 Elections[1]

2 November 2002: Mufti Mohd. Sayeed sworn in as the J&K Chief Minister; militants attack the Mufti's residence, killing a Congress leader (*The Hindu*, 3 November 2002).

5 November 2002: Mufti Sayeed asks Centre to start dialogue with all the elected representatives of J&K and those who did not participate in the elections (*The Hindu*, 6 November 2002).

24 November 2002: Militants attack the Raghunath temple the second time in six months killing nine persons and injuring forty-two (*The Hindu*, 25 November 2002).

20 December 2002: Militants kill Abdul Aziz Mir, People's Democratic Party Member of the Legislative Assembly, in Pampore town of South Kashmir (*The Hindu*, 21 December 2002).

21 December 2002: Four members of a family killed and three women injured when militants attack their house in Rebbon village, near Sopore (*The Hindu*, 22 December 2002).

29 December 2002: Mufti Sayeed announces devolution of powers to the Ladakh Autonomous Hill Development Council (LAHDC) of Leh district and says that Kargil would also get a similar council by June (*The Hindu*, 30 December 2002).

11 March 2003: Mufti Mohd. Sayeed says that the J&K Government has decided to disband the anti-militancy Special Operations Group, which faced allegations of human rights violations (*The Hindu*, 12 March 2002).

[1] This Time Line includes major events that took place in what India calls as 'Jammu & Kashmir' and does not include the happening inside on what Pakistan calls as 'Azad Kashmir'. The incidents are collated from reports which appeared in *The Hindu*.

16 April 2003: Five persons killed and twenty-six, including seven army personnel injured in two powerful landmine blasts in Pulwama and Doda districts of Jammu & Kashmir (*The Hindu*, 17 April, 2003).

25 May 2003: The Jamaat-e-Islami removes Syed Ali Shah Geelani, from the executive body (*The Hindu*, 26 May 2003).

28 June 2003: Two terrorists attacked the Sanjuwan Army Camp on the outskirts of Jammu city and killed twelve Army personnel while injuring seven persons (*The Hindu*, 29 June 2003).

12 July 2003: Omar Abdullah announces the National Conference's withdrawal from the National Democratic Alliance (*The Hindu*, 13 July 2003).

21 July 2003: Seven devotees, including a child killed and thirty-eight injured in two powerful explosions at Banganga near Katra (*The Hindu*, 22 July 2003).

22 July 2003: Militants attack an Army Camp in Jammu killing four officers (*The Hindu*, 23 July 2003).

12 August 2003: Musharraf offered ceasefire at the Line of Control if India was willing to reciprocate and reduce the strength of its forces in the Kashmir Valley and cease 'atrocities' in Jammu & Kashmir among other measures (*The Hindu*, 13 August 2003).

22 August 2003: APHC Chairman, Maulvi Abbas Ansari expresses willingness to hold talks with the Central Government (*The Hindu*, 23 August 2003).

27 August 2003: Vajpayee announces that doors are open for those who reject militancy and extreme positions (*The Hindu*, 28 August 2003).

6 September 2003: A car-bomb explosion at the Parimpora fruit and vegetable market in suburban Srinagar claimes six civilian lives (*The Hindu*, 7 September 2003).

7 September 2003: All Party Hurriyat Conference (APHC) splits (*The Hindu*, 8 September 2003).

15 September 2003: Geelani takes over as the chairman of his faction of the APHC (*The Hindu*, 16 September 2003).

31 October 2003: Sixteen persons killed in a grenade attack by militants on a camp of the Special Operations Group in Shopian, South J&K (*The Hindu*, 1 November 2003).

27 November 2003: Twelve people including four security personnel killed in an ambush by militants (*The Hindu*, 28 November 2003).

18 December 2003: Musharraf announces Pakistan that has left aside UN Resolutions on Kashmir and is prepared to meet India half way in a bid to resolve the fifty-six year old problem (*The Hindu*, 19 December 2003).

13 January 2004: L.K. Advani, Home Minister of India invites the Hurriyat for talks from 22 January (*The Hindu*, 14 January 2004).

16 January 2004: Hizb Commander Dar killed in an encounter with the Army in J&K (*The Hindu*, 17 January 2004).

22 January 2004: Advani meets APHC leaders and agrees to find an 'honourable and durable solution' to the Kashmir problem through dialogue, hoping that all forms of violence at all levels would end (*The Hindu*, 23 January 2004).

2 February 2004: A militant kills a Deputy Inspector-General of the J&K police soon after he offered Id prayers at a mosque (*The Hindu*, 3 February 2004).

27 February 2004: Mufti Mohd. Sayeed escapes an assassination attempt at a public meeting in Beerwah (*The Hindu*, 28 February 2004).

APPENDIX IV

India-Pakistan Official Joint Statements and Agreements since Lahore Summit, 1999

A. TEXT OF INDIA, PAKISTAN JOINT STATEMENT, 20 JUNE 2004

In accordance with the agreement between the Foreign Secretaries of India and Pakistan in February 2004, Expert-level talks on Nuclear Confidence Building Measures were held in New Delhi from 19–20 June 2004. Dr Sheel Kant Sharma, Additional Secretary (IO), headed the Indian delegation and Tariq Osman Hyder, Additional Secretary (UN and EC) led the Pakistan side.

The visiting Pakistani delegation also called on the External Affairs Minister, K. Natwar Singh, the National Security Adviser J.N. Dixit and Foreign Secretary Shashank.

The talks were held in a cordial and constructive atmosphere

Both sides:

Conscious of the need to promote a stable environment of peace and security between the two countries,

Recognizing that the nuclear capabilities of each other, which are based on their national security imperatives, constitute a factor for stability,

Committed to national measures to reduce the risks of accidental or unauthorized use of nuclear weapons under their respective controls and to adopt bilateral notification measures and mechanisms to prevent misunderstandings and misinterpretations,

Committed to work towards strategic stability

The existing hotline between the DGMOs would be upgraded, and secured.

A dedicated and secure hotline would be established between the two Foreign Secretaries, through their respective Foreign Offices to prevent misunderstandings and reduce risks relevant to nuclear issues.

Both countries will work towards concluding an Agreement with technical parameters on pre-notification of flight testing of missiles, a draft of which was handed over by the Indian side.

Each side reaffirmed its unilateral moratorium on conducting further nuclear test explosions unless, in exercise of national sovereignty, it decides that extraordinary events have jeopardized its supreme interests.

Both countries would continue bilateral discussions and hold further meetings to work towards the implementation of the Lahore MoU of 1999.

Both countries will continue to engage in bilateral consultations on security and non-proliferation issues within the context of negotiations of these issues in multilateral fora.

Both countries called for regular working level meetings to be held among all the nuclear powers to discuss issues of common concern.

Both sides agreed to report the progress of the talks to the respective Foreign Secretaries who would meet on 27-28 June 2004.

B. TEXT OF INDIA-PAKISTAN STATEMENT, 18 FEBRUARY 2004

The following is the full joint statement issued at the end of talks between the Pakistani and Indian foreign secretaries in Islamabad on Wednesday.

'The foreign secretaries of Pakistan and India met on 18 February 2004.

They reviewed and endorsed the agreement worked out at the Director General/Joint Secretary meetings on 16 and 17 February on the modalities and timeframe for discussion on all subjects on the agenda of the composite dialogue.

Both sides agreed that they would approach the composite dialogue with the sincere desire to discuss and arrive at a peaceful settlement of all bilateral issues, including Jammu & Kashmir to the satisfaction of both sides.

They reiterated their commitment to promote progress towards the common objective of peace, security and economic development for their people and for future generations.

They agreed to the following schedule of meetings

Foreign secretaries would meet in May/June, 2004, for talks on peace and security including Confidence Building Measures (CBM) and Jammu & Kashmir.

Talks on Siachen; Wullar Barrage; Sir Creek; terrorism and drug trafficking; economic and commercial cooperation; and promotion of friendly exchanges in various fields would be held at the already agreed levels, in July 2004.

The following technical-level meetings would be held earlier

Meeting between Director-General Pakistan Rangers and Inspector-General Border Security Force (of India) in March/April 2004.

Expert-level talks on nuclear confidence-building measures in the latter half of May 2004.

Committee on drug trafficking and smuggling in June 2004

They reviewed the existing links between the Director-Generals of military operations of Pakistan and India and agreed to consider further strengthening these contacts.

The Foreign Minister of Pakistan and the External Affairs Minister of India would meet in August 2004 to review overall progress.

This would be preceded by a one-day meeting of the Foreign Secretaries.'

C. INDIA-PAKISTAN JOINT PRESS STATEMENT, ISLAMABAD, 6 JANUARY 2004

The President of Pakistan and the Prime Minister of India met during the SAARC Summit in Islamabad.

The Indian Prime Minister while expressing satisfaction over the successful conclusion of the SAARC Summit appreciated the excellent arrangements made by the host country.

Both leaders welcomed the recent steps towards normalisation of relations between the two countries and expressed the hope that the positive trends set by the CBMs would be consolidated.

Prime Minister Vajpayee said that in order to take forward and sustain the dialogue process, violence, hostility and terrorism must be prevented. President Musharraf reassured Prime Minister Vajpayee that he will not permit any territory under Pakistan's control to be used to support terrorism in any manner. President Musharraf emphasised that a sustained and productive dialogue addressing all issues would lead to positive results.

To carry the process of normalisation forward, the President of Pakistan and the Prime Minister of India agreed to commence the process of the composite dialogue in February 2004. The two leaders are confident that the resumption of the composite dialogue will lead to peaceful settlement of all bilateral issues, including Jammu & Kashmir, to the satisfaction of both sides.

The two leaders agreed that constructive dialogue would promote progress towards the common objective of peace, security and economic development for our peoples and for future generations.

Islamabad
6 January 2004

D. THE LAHORE DECLARATION, 21 FEBRUARY 1999

The Prime Ministers of the Republic of India and the Islamic Republic of Pakistan
Sharing a vision of peace and stability between their countries, and of progress and prosperity for their peoples;

Convinced that durable peace and development of harmonious relations and friendly cooperation will serve the vital interests of the peoples of the two countries, enabling them to devote their energies for a better future;

Recognising that the nuclear dimension of the security environment of the two countries adds to their responsibility for avoidance of conflict between the two countries;

Committed to the principles and purposes of the Charter of the United Nations, and the universally accepted principles of peaceful co-existence;

Reiterating the determination of both countries to implementing the Simla Agreement in letter and spirit;

Committed to the objective of universal nuclear disarmament and non-proliferation;

Convinced of the importance of mutually agreed confidence building measures for improving the security environment;

Recalling their agreement of 23 September 1998, that an environment of peace and security is in the supreme national interest of both sides and that the resolution of all outstanding issues, including Jammu & Kashmir, is essential for this purpose;

Have agreed that their respective Governments:

- shall intensify their efforts to resolve all issues, including the issue of Jammu & Kashmir.
- shall refrain from intervention and interference in each other's internal affairs.

- shall intensify their composite and integrated dialogue process for an early and positive outcome of the agreed bilateral agenda.
- shall take immediate steps for reducing the risk of accidental or unauthorised use of nuclear weapons and discuss concepts and doctrines with a view to elaborating measures for confidence building in the nuclear and conventional fields, aimed at prevention of conflict.
- reaffirm their commitment to the goals and objectives of SAARC and to concert their efforts towards the realisation of the SAARC vision for the year 2000 and beyond with a view to promoting the welfare of the peoples of South Asia and to improve their quality of life through accelerated economic growth, social progress and cultural development.
- reaffirm their condemnation of terrorism in all its forms and manifestations and their determination to combat this menace.
- shall promote and protect all human rights and fundamental freedoms.

Signed at Lahore on the 21st day of February 1999.
Atal Behari Vajpayee—Prime Minister of the Republic of India
Muhammad Nawaz Sharif—Prime Minister of the Islamic Republic of Pakistan

E. JOINT STATEMENT, 21 FEBRUARY 1999

1. In response to an invitation by the Prime Minister of Pakistan, Mr Muhammad Nawaz Sharif, the Prime Minister of India, Shri Atal Behari Vajpayee, visited Pakistan from 20-21 February 1999, on the inaugural run of the Delhi-Lahore bus service.
2 The Prime Minister of Pakistan received the Indian Prime Minister at the Wagah Border on 20 February 1999. A banquet in honour of the Indian Prime Minister and his delegation was hosted by the Prime Minister of Pakistan at Lahore Fort, on the same evening. Prime Minister Atal Behari Vajpayee, visited Minar-e-Pakistan, Mausoleum of Allama Iqbal, Gurdwara Dera Sahib and Samadhi of Maharaja Ranjeet Singh. On 21 February, a civic reception was held in honour of the visiting Prime Minister at the Governor's House.
3. The two leaders held discussions on the entire range of bilateral relations, regional cooperation within SAARC, and issues of international concern. They decided that:

   (a) The two Foreign Ministers will meet periodically to discuss all issues of mutual concern, including nuclear related issues.
   (b) The two sides shall undertake consultations on WTO related issues with a view to coordinating their respective positions.

(c) The two sides shall determine areas of cooperation in Information Technology, in particular for tackling the problems of Y2K.
(d) The two sides will hold consultations with a view to further liberalising the visa and travel regime.
(e) The two sides shall appoint a two member committee at ministerial level to examine humanitarian issues relating to Civilian detainees and missing POWs.

4. They expressed satisfaction on the commencement of a bus service between Lahore and Delhi, the release of fishermen and civilian detainees and the renewal of contacts in the field of sports.
5. Pursuant to the directive given by the two Prime Ministers, the Foreign Secretaries of Pakistan and India signed a Memorandum of Understanding on 21 February 1999, identifying measures aimed at promoting an environment of peace and security between the two countries.
6. The two Prime Ministers signed the Lahore Declaration embodying their shared vision of peace and stability between their countries and of progress and prosperity for their peoples.
7. Prime Minister Atal Behari Vajpayee extended an invitation to Prime Minister Muhammad Nawaz Sharif, to visit India on mutually convenient dates.
8. Prime Minister Atal Behari Vajpayee, thanked Prime Minister Muhammad Nawaz Sharif for the warm welcome and gracious hospitality extended to him and members of his delegation and for the excellent arrangements made for his visit.

Lahore,
21 February 1999.

F. MEMORANDUM OF UNDERSTANDING, 21 FEBRUARY 1999

The following is the text of the Memorandum of Understanding signed by the Foreign Secretary, Mr K. Raghunath, and the Pakistan Foreign Secretary Mr Shamshad Ahmad, at Lahore on Sunday:

The Foreign Secretaries of India and Pakistan

Reaffirming the continued commitment of their respective governments to the principles and purposes of the U.N. Charter;

Reiterating the determination of both countries to implementing the Simla Agreement in letter and spirit;

Guided by the agreement between their Prime Ministers of 23 September 1998 that an environment of peace and security is in the supreme national interest of both sides and that resolution of all outstanding issues, including Jammu & Kashmir, is essential for this purpose;

Pursuant to the directive given by their respective Prime Ministers at Lahore, to adopt measures for promoting a stable environment of peace, and security between the two countries;

Have on this day, agreed to the following

The two sides shall engage in bilateral consultations on security concepts, and nuclear doctrines, with a view to developing measures for confidence building in the nuclear and coventional fields, aimed at avoidance of conflict.

The two sides undertake to provide each other with advance notification in respect of ballistic missile flight tests, and shall conclude a bilateral agreement in this regard.

The two sides are fully committed to undertaking national measures to reducing the risks of accidential or unauthorised use of nuclear weapons under their respective control. The two sides further undertake to notify each, other immediately in the event of any accidential, unauthorised or unexplained incident that could create the risk of a fallout with adverse consequences for both sides, or an outbreak of a nuclear war between the two countries, as well as to adopt measures aimed at diminishing the possibility of such actions, or such incidents being misinterpreted by the other. The two side shall identify/establish the appropriate communication mechanism for this purpose.

The two sides shall continue to abide by their respective unilateral moratorium on conducting further nuclear test explosions unless either side, in exercise of its national sovereignty decides that extraordinary events have jeopardised its supreme interests.

The two sides shall conclude an agreement on prevention of incidents at sea in order to ensure safety of navigation by naval vessels, and aircraft belonging to the two sides.

The two sides shall periodically review the implementation of existing CBMs and where necessary, set up appropriate consultative mechanisms to monitor and ensure effective implementation of these CBMs.

The two sides shall undertake a review of the existing communication links (e.g. between the respective Directors-General, Military Operations) with a view to upgrading and improving these links, and to provide for fail-safe and secure communications.

The two sides shall engage in bilateral consultations on security, disarmament and non-proliferation issues within the context of negotiations on these issues in multilateral fora.

Where required, the technical details of the above measures will be worked out by experts of the two sides in meetings to be held on mutually agreed dates, before mid 1999, with a view to reaching bilateral agreements.

Done at Lahore on 21 February 1999 in the presence of Prime Minister of India, Mr Atal Behari Vajpayee, and Prime Minister of Pakistan, Mr Muhammad Nawaz Sharif.

(*K. Raghunath*)
Foreign Secretary of the Republic of India

(*Shamshad Ahmad*)
Foreign Secretary of the Islamic Republic of Pakistan

Bibliography

NEWS REPORTS

'Advani Back to Pak-bashing, says ISI Spread all over India', *The Indian Express*, 12 November 1998.

'A Positive Gesture from Pakistani' (editorial), *The Hindu*, 14 January 2002.

'A Remarkable Visit: Pakistani Scribes', *The Hindu*, 10 October 2004.

'All Options are Open: PM', *The Hindu*, 20 December 2001.

'Army, BSF Lay Mines along the LoC', *The Hindu*, 4 January 2002.

'BJP Calls for Closure of Pakistan Mission', *The Hindu*, 9 February 2003.

'Book Fair a Success Story for Pak Publishers', *The Tribune*, 20 February 2004.

'Call for Freeing Indo-Pak Trade', *The Business Line*, 7 September 2001.

'Call for Improving Indo-Pak Trade', *Deccan Herald*, 3 March 2004.

'Centre Invites J&K Militants for Talks', *The Hindu*, 29 July 2000.

'Cricket and Politics' (editorial), *The Hindu*, 2 June 2001.

'Dead Bodies will be Retuned if Cricket Team Visits Pak', *The Hindu*, 7 February 2001.

'Dissidents Want Geelani at Helm', *Daily Excelsior*, 9 September 2003.

'Dr Khan Seeks Pardon', *Dawn*, 5 February 2004.

'Dr Qadeer Removed from Adviser Post', *The News*, 1 February 2004.

'Economics Must Play Dominant Role in Indo-Pak Ties: Sinha', *The Hindu*, 8 July 2003.

'Elections to Hurriyat Unconstitutional, says Geelani', *The Hindu*, 20 July 2003.

'Fazlur Rehman Reiterates LoC can Become Border', *Hindustan Times*, 19 July 2003.

'Fernandes Unveils "Limited War" Doctrine', *The Hindu*, 25 January 2000.

'Fillip to Indo-Pak Trade Overdue', *The Statesman*, 14 August 2001.

'First Batch of Passengers Arrives from Lahore', *The Hindu*, 17 March 1999.

'Foreign Secys Meet by March-end: Aziz', *The Hindu*, 25 February 1999.

'Full Steam Ahead on Iran Gas via Pak', *The Indian Express*, 25 October 2004.

'Gas Pipeline Project Hinges on MFN Status to India', *The Hindu*, 11 January 2004.

'Geelani Defies Jamaat', *The Hindu*, 27 June 2003.

'Geelani is an Indian Agent, Claims Lone', *Hindustan Times*, 9 July 2003.

'Geelani Plans a New Front', *Hindustan Times*, 30 June 2003.

'Government Decides to Punish Guilty Scientists', *The News*, 27 January 2004.

'Hawk Geelani tells Hurriyat: Take Harder Line or I Will Fly Away', *The Indian Express*, 5 July 2003.

'Help Offered to India on Gas Pipeline Project', *Dawn*, 14 July 2003.

'Hijack Plot was Hatched in Pak', *The Hindustan Times*, 23 January 2000;

'Hijackers are not our Nationals, says Pakistan', *The Times of India*, 3 January 2000.

'Hijackers Identified; Pak Hand Confirmed', *The Times of India*, 7 January 2000.

'Hostility Flares up during Indo-Pak Talks on Siachen', *The Times of India*, 7 November 1998.

'How India and Pakistan Broke the Ice', *Hindustan Times*, 8 January 2004.

'India and Pakistan Agree to Disagree Even on Water', *Economic Times*, 6 November 1998.

'India is Ready to Open Sindh Border', *The Asian Age*, 10 March 1999.

'India Keen on Transit Rights as Part of Pipeline Deal', *The Hindu*, 13 October 2004.

'India may Consider Gas Pipeline via Pak', *The Indian Express*, 5 June 2004.

'India Ready to Consider Gas Pipeline via Pakistan', *Dawn*, 3 January 2004.

'India Rejects Pak Move on Sir Creek Issue', *The Hindu*, 10 November 1998.

'India Rejects Proposal for Import of Gas via Pakistan', *Hindustan Times*, 12 December 2003.

'India Suggests Reunions for Kashmiri Families', *Daily Times*, 29 December 2004.

'India Wants Pak to be Declared a Terrorist State', *The Times of India*, 4 January 2000.

'India, Pak Agree on Calendar for Talks', *The Hindu*, 18 September 1998.

'India, Pak Agreement on Talks', *The Hindustan Times*, 4 September 1998.

'India, Pak to Continue Talks on Tulbul Project', *The Hindu*, 6 November 1998.

'India, Pak Exchange Prisoners', *The Hindu*, 23 March 1999.

'India, Pak to Free Civilian Prisoners', *The Hindu*, 7 March 1999.

'India, Pakistan Agree to Sustain Dialogue Process', *The Hindu*, 3 July 2004.

'Indian Team Arrives on Peace Mission, *Dawn*, 2 February 2004.

'Indian Track II Team Arriving in Pak', *Hindustan Times*, 19 January 2004.

'Indian, Pakistani MPs for Isolation of Fundamentalists', *Hindustan Times*, 9 May 2003.

'India's Missile System "in Position": Fernandes', *The Hindu*, 27 December 2001.

'Indo-Pak Bus Talks all Words, no Results', *The Tribune*, 9 December 2004.

'Indo-Pak Talk and Deadlock Continues', *The Economic Times*, 10 November 1998,

'Indo-Pak Track II Doves Moot 16 Points Peace Plan', *Hindustan Times*, 22 January 2004.

'Indo-Pak Tulbul Talks a Washout', *The Pioneer*, 6 November 1998.

'Indo-Pak Dialogue Must Go On', *The Hindu*, 20 March 1999.

'Jamali Raises Gas Pipeline Issue', *The Hindu*, 7 January 2004.

'Jammu & Kashmir Assembly Elections 2002: Under the Shadow of Fear', *Economic and Political Weekly*, 26 October 2002, pp. 4357-60.

'Kashmir Assembly Election: How Free and Fair?' *Economic and Political Weekly*, 11 January 2003, pp. 101-5.

'Kashmir: What Next', in *Defence, Technology and Cooperation in South Asia*, Report on the Proceeding of Tenth Workshop, 56–61 <http://www.rcss.org/summerboook.pdf>

'Let's Forget Modalities and Resume Talks: Aziz', *The Hindustan Times*, 3 September 1998.

'Little Headway in Talks on Bus Service', *The Hindu*, 8 December 2004.

'More Nuclear Scientists held for Questioning', *The News*, 19 January 2004.

'Musharraf to Discuss Cricket Relations', *The Hindu*, 1 June 2001.

'Natwar Singh, Kasuri Meeting "productive"', *The Hindu*, 22 June 2004.

'96 CBMs Exchanged by India, Pak since April 2003', *The Tribune*, 31 October 2004.

'No Breakthrough in Talks, says Pak', *The Hindu*, 2 September 1998.

'No Cricket with Pak: India', *The Hindu*, 8 December 2002.

'No Headway in Indo-Pak Talks on Sir Creek Dispute', *The Times of India*, 10 November 1998.

'No Road Map on Kashmir: Malik', *Greater Kashmir*, 18 June 2003.

'No Role for Pakistan: PM', *The Hindu*, 7 August 2000.

'Not Cricket! Sena Men Vandalise BCCI Office', *The Indian Express*, 20 January 1999.

'N-scientists Debriefing in National Interest: PM', *Dawn*, 23 January 2004.

'Nuclear Issue' (editorial) *The News*, 28 January 2004.

'Pak Bans Ties with Indian Universities', *The Asian Age*, 7 November 2001.

'Pak Grants Permission for Cricket Fans', *The Hindu*, 27 March 1999.

'Pak had "Prior Knowledge" of IA Plane Hijack', *The Hindu*, 10 January 2000.

'Pak-India Forum Disapproves of Visa Restrictions', *The Hindu*, 3 January 2003.

'Pak not Interested in Good Ties, says PM', *The Hindu*, 9 February 2003.

'Pak to Resort to "Other Means" If Talks Fail', *The Hindu*, 1 March 1999.

'Pak Role in Poliferation' (editorial), *the Nation*, 6 January 2004.

'Pak Threatens to Cut Cricket Ties', *The Asian Age*, 28 March 2001.

'Pak Writers Denied Visa', *The Hindu*, 12 January 2003.

'Pakistan Backs Iran-India Gas Pipeline', *The News*, 17 October 2003.

'Pakistan Directs Four Diplomats to Leave in 48 Hours', *The News*, 8 February 2003.

'Pakistan Envoy Asked to Leave India', *Hindustan Times*, 8 February 2003.

'Pakistan Gets New Year Card Full of CBMs', *Hindustan Times*, 1 January 2004.

'Pakistan Holds Scientists for Questioning', *The New York Times*, 13 December 2003.

'Pakistan Links Trade to Peace, Security', *The Times of India*, 11 November 1998.

'Pakistani Nuclear Commerce' (editorial), *The New York Times*, 23 December 2003.

'Pakistan Pledges 5750 Visas for the ODIs', *The Times of India*, 26 February 2004.

'Pakistan Questions 8 Connected to Its Nuclear Program', *The New York Times*, 19 January 2004.

'Pakistan Rejects India's Siachen Ceasefire Plan', *The Hindu*, 7 November 1998.

'Pakistan Scholars Pledge Peace, Not War', *The Asian Age*, 28 November 2000.

'Pakistan, India Fail to Resolve Tulbul Dispute': *The Times of India*, 6 November 1998.

'Pakistan's Nuclear Dealings, Rogues Step In', *The Economist* 370, no. 8357 (10 January 2004).

'Pakistani Scouts Attend SAARC Camp at Gulmarg', *The Hindu*, 6 July 2004.

'Passport-visa System Mooted for Srinagar-Muzaffarabad Bus Service', *The Hindu*, 21 January 2004.

'Peace First, then MFN Status', *The Asian Age*, 11 November 1998.

'Peace, Dialogue Figure in PM's Talks with Fazlur', *The Hindu*, 21 July 2003.

'Peace this Pipeline' (editorial), *The Indian Express*, 20 July 2004.

'Pipeline via Pak not Acceptable: India', *The Times of India*, 29 July 2003.

'PM Hails Ceasefire Offer', *The Hindu*, 26 July 2000.

'PM Talks Pak, Peace and Prosperity in J&K', *The Times of India*, 18 April 2003.

'Positive Development: Hizbul', *The Hindu*, 30 July 2000.

'RSS Backs Vajpayee's Peace Bid with Pakistan', *Hindustan Times*, 2 May 2003.

'RSS Chief to Visit Pakistan?' *The Hindu*, 15 August 2000.

'Salahuddin Sets August 8 Deadline for Tripartite Talks', *The Hindu*, 4 August 2000.

'Security Forces Told not to Jeopardize Ceasefire', *The Hindu*, 27 July 2000.

'Sena Forms "Suicide Squad" ', *The Tribune*, 20 January 1999.

'Sena not for Cricketing Ties with Pak', *The Hindu*, 24 March 2001.

'Should we Liberalise Visas for Pakistanis?' *The Times of India*, 30 December 2000.

'Siachen Issue will be Discussed Afresh', *The Asian Age*, 6 November 1998.

'Siachen Talks Go the Tulbul Way', *The Hindustan Times*, 7 November 1998.

'Siachen War of Words Stings India', *The Telegraph*, 7 November 1998.

'Sir Creek: Talks Fail, Pak for Arbitration', *The Indian Express*, 10 November 1998.

'Soften Borders, say Pakistani scribes', *The Hindu*, 5 October 2004.

'Strike Forces Moved Closer to the Border', *The Hindu*, 21 December 2001.

'Talks Likely on Troop Pullout', *The Hindustan Times*, 18 March 1999.

Talks Offer a "Blunder": Singhal', *The Hindu*, 26 April 2003.

Text of Joint Statement Issued at Indo-Pak Talks Conclusion, *Pakistan Times*, 5-6 September 2004 <http://www.pakistantimes.net/2004/09/09/top11.htm>

'The Right Approach' , editorial, *Dawn*, 6 December 2004.

'Throw Open Wagah, There will be Traffic Jams', *The Hindu*, 3 May 2000.

'Ties May Worsen, says Islamabad', *Dawn*, 9 February 2003.

'Tough Talks Replaces Bonhomie', *The Pioneer*, 1 March 99.

'Track II Diplomacy Back on Track', *The Nation*, 20 January 2004.

'Trade Ties Linked to Political Breakthrough', *The Telegraph*, 11 November 1998.

'Visiting Indian MPs Baffled by Pak Govt's Indifference', *The Times of India*, 23 June 2003.

'War of Words Stalls Indo-Pak Dialogue', *The Asian Age*, 2 March 1999.

'We Could Take a Strike and Survive, Pakistan won't: Fernandes', *Hindustan Times*, 30 December 2001.

'We have Evidence against Pak, says Brajesh', *The Hindu*, 3 January 2000.

'We Support the Path of Peace, says Fazlur Rehman', *The Hindu*, 19 July 2003.

'We will not Loose any more Territory, says PM', *The Hindu*, 1 March 1999.

BOOKS AND ARTICLES

Agha, Ayesha Siddqa, 'Dealing with Nuclear Bureaucracies in South Asia', *The Friday Times*, 9-15 January 2004.

Ahmed, Firdaus, 'The Impetus behind Limited War', *Peace and Conflict*, vol. 6, no. 2 (2003).

Akhtar, Shaheen, 'IHK State Assembly Elections 2002', *Regional Studies*, vol. XXII, no. 2, Spring 2003, pp. 33–43 and *Regional Studies*, vol. XXII, no. 3, Summer 2003, pp. 71–135.

Albright, David and Holly Higgins, 'A Bomb for Ummah', *Bulletin of Atomic Scientists*, March–April 2003.

Aneja, Atul, 'Pakistan had Three-phased Plan?' *The Hindu*, 23 June 1999.

Baabar, Mariana, 'Pakistan Smiling', *Outlook*, 29 March 2004.

Baker, Peter, 'Pakistani Scientist who Met bin Laden Failed Polygraphs', *Washington Post*, 3 March 2002.

Baruah, Amit, 'India Proposes a Dozen Steps to Break the Ice with Pak', *The Hindu*, 23 October 2003.

Bhushan, Bharat, 'High Altitude War that is Most Wasteful and Futile', *The Hindustan Times*, 6 November 1998.

Bidwai, Praful, 'Why War is no Option', *Hindustan Times*, 20 December 2001.

Bokhari, Farhan, 'Nuclear Questions', *The News*, 29 January 2004.

Broad, William J. David E. Sanger and Raymond Bonner, 'A Tale of Nuclear Proliferation: How Pakistani Built His Network', *The New York Times*, 12 February 2004.

Bunn, George et al., 'Strengthening Nuclear Security', *Non Proliferation Review*, Fall/Winter 2001.

Chandran, Suba and Rizwan Zeb, 'Taking the Indo-Pak Peace Process Further', *IPCS Policy Brief 2*, March 2004.

Chandran, Suba, 'All Parties Hurriyat Confusion: Implications of an Exit', <http://www.ipcs.org/ipcs/issueIndex2.jsp?action=showView&kValue= 1106&issue=1012&status=article&mod=b>

———, 'Why Kargil: Pakistan's Objectives and Motivations', in Maj. Gen. Ashok Krishna and P.R. Chari, eds., *Kargil: The Tables Turned* (New Delhi: Manohar, 2001).

———, *Limited War: Revisiting Kargil in the Indo-Pak Conflicts* (New Delhi: India Research Press, 2005).

Chari, P.R., 'Command and Control Arrangements' <http://www.ipcs.org/issues/articles/135-ndi-chari.html>

———, 'India's New Peace Initiative', IPCS Website, 24 October 2003, <http://www.ipcs.org/India_Pak_articles2.jsp?action=showView&kValue=1201&status=article&mod=a>

Cheema, Zafar Iqbal, 'Pakistan's Nuclear Use Doctrine and Command and Control', in Peter Lavoy et al., *Planning the Unthinkable: How New Powers will use Nuclear, Biological and Chemical Weapons* (Ithaca: Cornell University Press, 2000).

Chellaney, Brahma, 'India puts Musharraf in his Place', *Hindustan Times*, 14 January 2002.

Cohen, Stephen P., 'India, Pakistan and Kashmir', *Journal of Strategic Studies*, vol. 25, no. 4, December 2002.

———, 'Testimony Before the Senate Foreign Relations Committee on India and Pakistan: Steps Towards Rapprochement', 28 January 2004 <http://www.brookings.edu/dybdocroot/views/testimony/cohens/20040128.pdf>

David E. Sanger and William J. Broad, 'Pakistani's Nuclear Earnings: $ 100 Million', *The New York Times*, 16 March 2004.

Dixit, J.N., 'Invasion of Kargil', *Hindustan Times*, 23 June 1999.

Dixit, J.N., 'Untying the Gordian Knot', *The Hindustan Times*, 19 August 1998.

Fernandes, George, 'The Dynamics of Limited War', <http://www.stratmag.com/issueOct-15/page07.htm>

Hajni, Mehraj and Ravinderjit Kaur, 'Mufti Government: Promises and Performances', *Peace and Conflict*, 7, no. 3, March 2004.

Hoagland, Jim, 'Pakistan's Nuclear Alibaba', *The Washington Post*, 10 February 2004.

Huqqani, Hussain, 'India Should Make Diplomacy, Not War', *The Indian Express*, 20 December 2001.

Hussain, Syed Muzammil, 'Srinagar-Muzaffarabad Bus Service', *The News*, 18 November 2003.

Irshad, Muhammad, 'Vajpayee's Hand of Friendship', *Defence Journal*, Karachi, June 2003, <www.defencejournal.com/2003/june/vajpayeehand off riend ship.htm>

Kargil Review Committee Report, *From Surprise to Reckoning* (New Delhi: Sage Publications, 2000).

Khan, Kamran and Molly Moore, '2 Nuclear Scientists Briefed bin Laden, Pakistanis Say', *Washington Post*, 12 December 2001.

Khan, Tanvir Ahmad, 'Command and Control: A Pakistani Perspective', *Strategic Issues*, March 2000.

Khosa, Aasha, 'Track II Diplomacy: Pak Ulema to Visit India', *The Indian Express*, 25 May 2001.

Kumar, Amitava, 'The Enemy Within', *Herald* (Karachi), August 2001.

Lama, Mahendra P., 'Boosting Indo-Pak Trade', *The Hindustan Times*, 1 January 1999.

Malhotra, Inder, 'Gas Pipelines via Pakistan', *The Tribune*, 22 July 2004.

Masood, Talat, 'Kashmir and Indo-Pak Conflict', *South Asian Journal*, no. 1, August-September 2003.

Masoodi, Amin, 'Mufti Government and the Healing Touch', <http://www.ipcs.org/Kashmir_articles2.jsp?action=showView&kValue=1135&issue=1012&status=article&mod=a>

Mattoo, Amitabh, 'The Valley is Elsewhere', *The Indian Express*, 6 January 2000.

Mazari, Shireen, 'India's Peace Dilemma', *Strategic Studies*, vol. XXIV, no. 4, Winter 2004.

———, 'The Kargil Conflict 1999 Seperating Facts from Fictions', Islamabad: ISSI, 2003.

Mcgeary, Johanna, 'Inside the A-Bomb Bazaar', *Time* 163, no. 2 (19 January 2004).

Mehra, S.K., 'Kashmir Issue-I', *The Statesman* (New Delhi), 7 July 1998.

Mehta, Ashok K., 'Shifting Policies Deter Military Resolve', *The Pioneer*, 4 January 2002.

Mitchell, Christopher R., 'Cutting Losses: Reflections on Appropriate Timing', ICAR Working Paper 9, January 1996, <http://www.ciaonet.org/wps/mic01>

Mooradian, Moorad and Daniel Druckman, 'Hurting Stalemate or Mediation? The Conflict over Nagorno-Karabakh, 1990-95', *Journal for Peace Research*, vol. 36, no. 6.

Pachauri, R.K., 'Air Indo-Pak Peace in the Pipeline?' *The Times of India*, 5 February 2004.

Patnaik, Elisa, 'Tourism Slowly Picking up in Kashmir', *The Asian Age*, 13 September 1998.

Pregenzer, Arian L., 'Securing Nuclear Capabilities in India and Pakistan', *Non Proliferation Review*, Spring 2003.

Qadir, Shaukat, 'An Analysis of the Kargil Conflict', *RUSI Journal* (April 2002).

Raja Mohan, C., 'Between War and Peace', *The Hindu*, 20 December 2001.

———, 'Inviting Benazir Bhutto?' *The Hindu*, 1 February 2001.

———, 'The Time is Now', *The Hindu*, 13 January 2002.

———, 'Vajpayee's Speech, a Bid to Regain Initiative', *The Hindu*, 19 April 2003.

Reddy, Rammanohar C., 'The Cost of War', *The Hindu*, 5 January 2002.

Sabur, A.K.M. Abdus, 'Indo-Pakistan Security Relationship and the Kargil Crisis', *BIIS Journal*, vol. 20, no. 3, 1999.

Saleem, Farrukh, 'Our Nuclear Quagmire', *The Friday Times*, 2-8 January 2004.

Sanger, David E. and William J. Broad, 'From Rogue Nuclear Programs, Web of Trails Leads to Pakistan', *The New York Times*, 4 January 2004.

Sawant, Gaurav C., 'War with no Winners', *The Indian Express*, 7 November 1998.

Sehzad, Mohammad, 'The Solution Is Simple', *Dawn*, 14 September 2003.

Shahi, Agha, 'Command and Control of Nuclear Weapons in South Asia', *Strategic Issues*, March 2000.

Singh, Jasjit, 'Dynamics of Limited War', *Strategic Analysis* (October 2000).

———, 'Not Pipedreams', *The Indian Express*, 23 July 2003.

Steinberg, Gerald M., 'Unripeness and Conflict Management: Re-examining the Oslo Process and its Lessons', <http://faculty.biu.ac.il/~steing/conflict/papers re-examiningoslo.htm>

Subrahmanyam, K., 'Indo-Pak Nuclear Conflict Unlikely', *The Times of India*, 2 January 2002.

Swami, Praveen, 'A Catalogue of Crime', *Frontline*, 30 January–12 February 1999.

———, 'A Ceasefire in Kashmir', *Frontline*, 5-18 August 2000.

———, 'Fissures in the Hizb', *Frontline*, 26 April-9 May 2003.

———, 'Hurriyat Chairman Deposed, Claim Dissidents', *The Hindu*, 8 September 2003.

———, 'Spreading its Wings', *Frontline*, 16–29 January 1999.

Tyler, Patrick E. and David E. Sanger, 'Pakistan Called Libyan's Source of Atom', *The New York Times*, 6 January 2004.

Weiss, Leonard, 'Pakistan: It's Deja Vu All Over Again', *Bulletin of the Atomic Scientists* (May-June 2004).

Wirsing, Robert G., *Kashmir in the Shadow of War: Regional Rivalries in a Nuclear Age* (Armonk, NY: M.E. Sharpe, 2003).

Zartman, William, 'Ripeness: The Hurting Stalemate and Beyond', in *International Conflict Resolution after the Cold War*, ed. Paul Stern and Daniel Druckman (Washington: National Academy Press, 2000).

Zeb, Rizwan, 'Peace Process and the News Media: A Closer Look at the Agra Summit', *Regional Studies*, vol. XXI, no. 2, Spring 2003.

———, 'Can the Indo-Pak Peace Process be Saved?' <http://www.ipcs.org/newKashmirLevel2.jsp?action=showView&kValue=1437&subCatID=null&mod=null>

———, 'From War to Peace: Will it Last?', <http://www.ipcs.org/newKashmirLevel2.jsp?action=showView&kValue=1303&subCatID=null&mod=null>

Zehra, Nasim, 'Why did it Work at Islamabad, *The News*, 8 January 2004.

RCSS PUBLICATIONS

- *Defence, Technology and Cooperative Security in South Asia: Report on the Proceedings of the Tenth Summer Workshop* (RCSS, 2004)
- *Environment Development and Human Security: Perspectives from South Asia* (2003)
- *Terrorism in South Asia: Impact on Development and Democratic Process* (SIPRA, 2003)
- *South Asia and the War on Terrorism* (India Research Press, 2003)
- *Shaping the Future—A South Asian Civil Society Dialogue* (RCSS, July 2002)
- *Small Arms and Human Insecurity* (RCSS, July 2002)
- *SAARC in the Twenty-First Century: Towards a Cooperative Future* (July 2002)
- *Memories of a Genocidal Partition: The Haunting Tale of Victims, Witnesses and Perpetrators* (RCSS, July 2002)
- *South Asian Security Futures: A Dialogue of Director's Regional Strategic Studies Institutes* (March 2002)
- *Security and Governance in South Asia* (September 2001)
- *Globalization and Non-Traditional Security in South Asia* (September 2001)
- *Security in the New Millennium* (India Research Press, 2001)
- *The Simla Agreement 1972—Its Wasted Promise* (Manohar, 2001)

RCSS Newsletter

A quarterly bulletin, it publishes a brief report of RCSS activities, presentations at its workshops on topics of contemporary interest and news and programmes of the RCSS and its alumnae.

RCSS Policy Studies

35 Nuclear Risk Reduction Measures in South Asia: Problems and Prospects (Manohar, 2005)
34 Indo-Pak Conflicts: Ripe to Resolve? (Manohar, 2005)
33 Small Arms and the Security Debate in South Asia (Manohar, 2005)
32 New Nuclear Triangle and China's Role in South Asia (forthcoming)
31 Stability through Economic Cooperation in a Nuclear Environment (Manohar, 2005)
30 Multi-Track Diplomacy between India and Pakistan: A Conceptual Framework for Sustainable Security (Manohar, 2005)
29 The Role of Mediation in Resolving India-Pakistan Conflict: Parameters and Possibilities (Manohar, 2005)
28 HIV/AIDS as a Security Threat to India (Manohar, 2005)
27 Nepal's Maoist Movement and Implications for India and China (Manohar, 2005)
26 Elite Perceptions in Foreign Policy: Role of Print Media in Influencing India-Pakistan Relations, 1989–1999 (Manohar, 2004)
25 Nuclar Risk Reduction Measures and Restraint Regime in South Asia (Manohar, 2004)
24 River Water Sharing Problem Between India and Pakistan: Case Study of the Indus Basin Water Treaty (June 2004)
23 Christianity and Political Conflict in India: The Case of Gujarat (June 2002)

Fellowship in South Asian Alternatives (FISAA) Monograph

- Water, Power And People: A South Asian Manifesto on the Politics and Knowledge of Water (1997)
- The Nuclear Debate: Ironies and Immoralities (1998)

Others

- *Directory of Individuals and Institutions Engaged in South Asian Strategic Studies* (1998).